MINDFUL
SUCCESS™

MINDFUL SUCCESS™

HOW TO USE YOUR MIND TO TRANSFORM YOUR LIFE

Magie Cook

Wisdom
Book

ACKNOWLEDGEMENTS

In making the creation of this book possible, I am very grateful and thankful for all of the people that came into my life and helped me achieve this goal. I express my sincere gratitude and thanks to:

Gary Reid with The Jack Canfield Coaching Program, for inspiring me to write this book and helping me rediscover my life's purpose during a very difficult time in my life. Thank you for uplifting me and believing in me through my process of self-rediscovery. Thank you to Walter Rahim Olden, owner of Pronomical Marketing, who came into my life in perfect timing, helping me publish this book and making Maggie's Salsa LLC, Magie Cook LLC and all of its products a marketing success. You are an amazing Spiritual being. I am so grateful and thankful that you came into my life. I see so much greatness in you and I can't wait to see where our journey takes us. Thank you to my dearest

i

friend Sarah K. Slocum for helping me proofread this book before publishing it. You have been an amazing friend for over a decade. I love your spirit and who you really are, always a fun and playful soul. Even though you live so far away, you are such a joy to be around every time I see you. I would like to extend a special thank you to my book editor Melissa Peitsch and formatting agent Mercedes Tabano II for your much-appreciated work in making this book a print success. I send everyone here my sincere and deepest blessings, and I look forward to working with you again in my future successful book projects.

May this book be a great blessing as well as the preparer of the fertile soil (your mind) for the seeds (the message) that will inspire and transform people's lives.

DEDICATION

This book is dedicated to my father, Dr. John Charles Cook-Lawson, who was a missionary in rural Mexico for four decades. A man who cared for the poor so deeply that he gave everything he had to inspire, heal, and feed thousands, to my mother, Maria Lucia Garcia Romero De Cook, for her dedicated work of caring for hundreds of abandoned and abused children at the Mano De Ayuda Orphanage and Clinic, to my biological brothers and sisters who endured in poverty and tremendous suffering along with me, Lucia De Jesus, Soledad De Getsemeni, Juan Gaspar, Mariana Caridad, Francisco Nazario, Maria Natividad, Josue, to all of my 68 legally adoptive brothers and sisters who lived with us, and the rest of the 200 and more kids who came to live at the orphanage since 1979. May this book help you heal your wounds from the past, and inspire and transform your life so that you can achieve ultimate happiness and live the life that you truly deserve, a heaven here on earth.

My Family

This book is also dedicated to YOU. May its gifts of wisdom help you discover the truth about *who you really are* and the power you possess to become limitless!

CONTENTS

ACKNOWLEDGMENTS   i

INTRODUCTION   1

THE SECRETS TO ALL SUCCESS   7

1   Remember Who You Are   9

-   *Magie, Go Put on a Dress!*   11
-   *Your Inner Kingdom*   17
-   *My Purpose Revealed*   20

2   The Universal Law   23

-   *Instant Manifestation*   31
-   *The Art of Allowing*   34
-   *There Are No Accidents*   36

3   Not Only Thoughts Become Things   43

-   *Choosing Happiness*   44
-   *Seeing Into Being*   58
-   *The Beggar*   63

4   The Mind   65

-   *Don't Touch!*   69
-   *Feelings in Words*   70
-   *Influence*   72

5   Got Faith?   77

-   *Living by Faith*   87
-   *A New Beginning*   91
-   *Being Homeless*   94
-   *The AHA Moment*   96

6   Perseverance   101

-   *"No" is Never Forever*   102
-   *A Piece of Wood Block*   107

7   Inspired Action   109

-   *Become It to Manifest It*   110

8 Mindful Goals   115

- *Take the First Step*   116
- *Believing in You!*   117
- *Living Your Purpose*   119
- *Writing Successful Goals*   129
- *Daily Success Goals*   132
- *100 Lifetime Goals*   138
- *Major Breakthrough Goal*   142

9 Vision Boards   147

- *The Power!*   147

10 Mindful Affirmations   153

- *Creative Magic!*   154

11 Mindful Meditations   161

- *My Greatest Miracle!*   162

SUFFERING & RELEASING YOUR BREAKS   165

12 Personal Success Blocks   167

- *Tough Love*   175
- *Forgiveness & Love*   177
- *Acceptance*   184

13 Hereditary Success Blocks   191

- *Emotional Poison*   195

14 Gratitude   197

- *Acknowledging Past Successes*   200
- *Remember Where You Came From*   204

15 Your Health & Success   215

- *Enjoy Now!*   219

REFERENCES & RESOURCES   229

INTRODUCTION

The Origin of This Book

I started writing this book a decade ago. I had been trying to write about my fascinating life experiences and the wisdom I have obtained along the way, but every time I sat down to write I could not get past a certain number of pages. I was haunted even stronger than before by all of the suffering that I experienced as I was growing up, even though I had lived those experiences so long ago. Everything that came out on paper were horrible memories, and occurrences of abuse, neglect, and fear. All of my stories of my early childhood were described so vividly that the negative impact of them set me immediately into a deep depression that kept me from writing.

One evening before going to bed, I was given a message through one of my meditations. The message said that in order to write the book that would inspire and transform people's lives, I had to go within and resolve all of these issues from my past. The moment that I began to write effortlessly was when I made the decision to *understand*, *forgive*, and *accept* my parents and all of the kids that lived in the orphanage for everything that I saw and experienced with them which had a negative impact my life. I made a choice to refrain from writing about the negative aspects that I lived through and dismiss all of my vivid recollections of suffering. I chose to focus on every positive aspect of my life experiences and what I did to create a successful and prosperous life in spite of the circumstances.

This book is all about INSPIRATION. From growing up in an orphanage where I experienced living in poverty and enduring suffering, to becoming homeless in the United States, to creating a multimillion-dollar brand with only $800 without getting in debt. This book contains fascinating success stories about the life lessons that I have learned along the way as well as a number of success principles, methods and personal tools that I used to create and transform my life. Everything that I have ever accomplished has not only been due to my own personal power, but the GREATER POWER that exists within us all which is the Spiritual Force and Power of God. This GREATER POWER has shown itself to me, it has manifested itself into my life, it has given me a message for you. This GREATER POWER wants you to know that it wants to manifest itself into your life as well, and that all you have to do is open the door to your heart and mind, and experience the fruits of the Spirit that have been prepared for you in this book.

Your natural birthright is abundance. God's ultimate purpose for you is to experience his kingdom NOW (in this moment) which is the source of all happiness joy, peace and abundance, letting go of all suffering that binds you so that you can live in eternal bliss.

MAGIE COOK

4

You are reading this book because you want to discover, understand, and apply its knowledge to achieve success in your life, whether it is personal, in business, health, wealth, or in relationships.

The basic understanding of *who you really are* is the basis for success that begins in your mind. In the following chapters, different unique ideas and principles for success will be revealed. I encourage you to study them and to try them and see which ones work best for you. You are a unique and wonderful Spiritual being. What works for you may not work for everyone else, so please take your time in discovering the best tools to use to transform your life.

Do not be conformed to this world, but be transformed by the renewal of your mind, that by testing you may discern what is the will of God, what is good and acceptable and perfect. Romans 12:2

MAGIE COOK

THE SECRETS TO ALL SUCCESS

1

Remember who you are

Do you realize how lucky you are? Do you know how blessed you are just for being here, for being born into an experience in which you have the freedom to express yourself and create whatever it is that you desire? You lucky salt!

Your existence is the greatest success you hold. You are a Divine Spiritual manifestation in this dream that you call life on earth. With this gift, you have the opportunity to create your own unique exhilarating experience, and to manifest anything that you desire; but first, you must remember *who you really are.*

Reality is merely an illusion, albeit a very persistent one.
— Albert Einstein

You must take a moment and put aside the worldly perception of you, which is an illusion based on what you perceive. You are so much more than just flesh and bones, so much more than what you see with your eyes. The truth is, you are a beautiful, magnificent, transcendent, and powerful Divine Being. Your eternal consciousness pervades your body and mind. The light of your true self is Pure Spirit, Source Energy, One with God, one with all that exists. You are a deliberate Divine creator who has chosen to be here in this dream of life, to grow, to expand, and to experience all of the wonderful joys of this earthly creation, so that you can participate in the creation process of your own expansion.

"We are not human beings having a spiritual experience.
We are spiritual beings having a human experience."
— Pierre Teilhard de Chardin

It is true that *believing* in yourself is the first secret to success, but believing in *who you really are* will give you limitless transcendental power to create and manifest in this lifetime what most people see as realistically impossible.

What if we were so passionate about remembering *who we really are*, each and every single day? We would be connected to our Higher Self, we would live at *Peace*, we would be full of *Love* and *Joy*, we would live with *Awareness* knowing what we know, and we would be free from the experience of suffering.

MAGIE, GO PUT ON A DRESS!

When I was growing up in my parent's orphanage in Mexico, I was not like the rest of the girls in the home. I grew up with the boys. I did everything with them. I played with them, worked with them in the fields, dressed like them, even showered with them. I was 10 years old at the time, and I had done something that required my father's discipline upon me. To my surprise, he figured out a very clever way to do it. He said, "Magie, go put on a dress!" Wow! That was it for me! I had never worn a dress before, and the first thing I thought was "oh no! I don't want to change; I just want to be me!" I was also afraid that my brothers would treat me differently, that they would not accept me, and I was terrified! In their eyes, I was strong, courageous, and respected. Even my older brothers looked up to me. So I held a meeting with all of my brothers, where I stood in the center of a circle and said to them, almost in tears, "Even though I am wearing this dress, and I don't look like me, I want you guys to know that I am still the same me deep down inside; I am still Magie." They all said, "Yes Magie!" and as they walked by me, they all gave me a firm punch on my shoulder, confirming their support for me. Then I took a knife and sliced my dress in the front and back between my legs, got on my horse bareback, and raced him towards the mountains to be by myself for a while. My father always had too much fun with this. When I was older, he never stopped laughing and talking about how it worked. It certainly taught me one lesson, and that was to remember **who I really was**. *In spite of the difficult situation I was in, I declared who I was, and I affirmed it to myself and everyone else. I was passionate about staying true to myself.*

This is who I really was

My first dress

Whether you want to say that it is God, Source Energy, The Universe, or whatever you wish to call the powerful Spiritual force that moves within us, the simple truth to be aware of is that we are all ONE in Spirit (one with God in real nature). We are one with and part of the creation process and expansion of this vast and limitless Universe that is always in motion. Because we are all One in Spirit, we are all connected. There is NO SPACE BETWEEN US AND GOD. Not even the air you are breathing right now. Wow! That is the most powerful awakening and understanding to live by. This means that every breath you take, and every step you take, God is always with you and you are always with God. When your eyes see, they see through the eyes of God, they see God in every human being, and it does not matter who they are, whether they are rich or poor, healthy or sick, or if they appear to be good or bad. They see God in all nature, they see God in every animal, they see God in everything that exists, and you are so grateful and thankful that you can see with the eyes of God, the eyes of knowledge. You feel exhilarated Joy, a deep sense of Inner Peace, and inexhaustible Unconditional Love for absolutely everything   that exists.

Being in Spirit is having *Awareness*, is feeling Unconditional Love, expressing Joy, and manifesting

Inner Peace. In Spirit, you are in control. When you connect to your true self, you have access to infinite power, boundless wisdom, and divine intelligence. Everything that you need to know is available to you, and the answer to every problem lies within your Subconscious mind. You are absolutely limitless!

In Spirit there is no suffering, there is no guilt, no resentment, no anger, no blame, and there is nothing to fear, not even fear itself. Nothing disturbs your Peace; you are complete. When you surrender all those beliefs about who you are not, and acknowledge *who you really are,* you no longer suffer; when you surrender to the real you, you surrender to God.

I tell you the truth, anyone who has faith in me will do what I have been doing. He will do even greater things than these, because I am going to the Father. John 14:12

Jesus was one of the wisest and most influential men that ever lived. What gave him his marvelous power was the understanding that God and man are One in real nature.

When Jesus refers to the Father, saying, "The Father that dwelleth in me" (John 14:10), and "I and the Father are One" (John 10:30), he was talking about Unity; he was talking about Oneness with God. The same "Unity" exists in the connection to all that is, all that exists, the "I AM that I AM" (Exodus 3:14), the same Father that lives within me, and you. See, we are three parted beings. Just as there are The Father, The Son and The Holy Ghost, there are Spirit, Soul and Body, and Cause, Medium, and Effect. All three form a Unity, a Oneness with God that makes us *who we really are*. In John 14:12, Jesus is telling you how powerful you are as a Spiritual being, how you could do even greater things than he did, if you believe in the greatness of *who you really are* in "Unity" with God, and in your connection to all that is, which is also God, who is everywhere and within everything that exists.

Nothing will ever compare to being here, having this earthly experience. We are magical, powerful, limitless, and amazing Divine creators. Do you know what "limitless" means? It means you get the opportunity to decide everything! We all have God's power within us, and to access it, we must go within, we must quiet our minds, and we must be still. When you access this power, when you tune into it, you leave the limitations of this earth and enter into another dimension of limitless that allows you to create and attract to yourself whatever it is that you want or need in this journey. You realize that this world we live in is an illusion, and you are no longer affected by it.

YOUR INNER KINGDOM

The Kingdom of Heaven is within you. Once you have learned how to enter your inner kingdom, you have a special retreat within that is always available to you"
-Dr. Wayne W. Dyer

The greatest secret in the world is that the kingdom of God is within us. You can access your inner kingdom anytime, and anywhere, through prayer and meditation. This is a place of complete peace and joy, a place where you can quiet your mind, connect with and speak to God, re-energize your spirit, clear your personal blocks caused by limiting beliefs, find a deep sense of love, search for guidance and revelation, and basically ask for anything that you desire. It is the birthplace of all of your life's attractions. This is your heaven, your oasis. In your inner kingdom, there is no suffering, only love, and you feel complete. Here you will find that your birthright is abundance, and your true nature is to live in a state of happiness. In this place, fear does not exist; it is only when you come out of your inner kingdom that you see fear and suffering all around you. It is important to go within and, as much as you can, to remain centered and in love. Going within is experiencing your true nature, it is experiencing *who you really are*, and it is experiencing Oneness with God.

I practice many forms of meditation based upon what my needs are, and what makes me truly exhilarated and happy in the moment. Prayer and meditation should be a peaceful and joyful process that allows you to quiet your mind and connect to God. You should never feel forced into doing something; if you do, you create resistance, and when you resist something, you always attract more of it.

I love to create my own forms of meditation and let God's power flow through me when I practice them. You can do the same. You can basically write a script on a powerful idea of how you want your meditation to flow, and then embark on your exhilarated inner journey. *If you are new to meditation, you can learn more about this subject by visiting our website at MeditationCreator.com.*

One of my favorite things to do each morning is to remember who I really am in Spirit. I take the time to quiet my mind and visualize how powerful I am as a creator. I visualize the light of God entering through my head and flowing into my body. I visualize this light becoming so strong that it wants to burst out of my body. I stand in the center of our manufacturing plant and visualize the light of God that has been building within me, flowing out of me in full force, and covering every square inch of our facility. Then I visualize this light also touching every team member that we have, and all of the products they make, every supermarket that carries them, and all of the people that buy them. I do the same thing with my home! This process is so real and powerful, so exhilarating and uplifting! I can always feel that there is a very good energy flowing in my home and workplace. I do this because it energizes me; I do this because I know the power of what I am creating each and every single day.

MY PURPOSE REVEALED

The very first time I connected with my higher self was when I was 7 years old. It was a Sunday afternoon, and my father had finished giving medical consultations to his patients at the orphanage's clinic. As we were walking out of the clinic, he stopped me and said to me, "Magie, look at these people" (it was a mother and her two small children walking out of the clinic), he grabbed me by the head with both of his hands and gave me a tight squeeze, and as he began to sob he said, "I never want you to be like this…I love these people." By looking at them, you could tell that these people were the poorest of the poor. They had nothing at all. He then proceeded to walk towards them, and I heard him gently say, "Here is a little bit of money for you to get back home and to buy yourself a taco." At that moment, I felt this powerful sensation all over my body and had the urge to look up to the sky and I heard a voice as if someone was speaking aloud to me that said, "You are destined for something big, you will change the lives of millions of people."

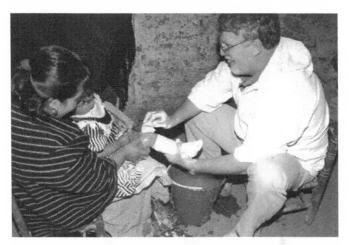

My father fixing a baby's clubbed feet

MAGIE COOK

2

The Universal Law

Our entire Spiritual Universe operates by law; just like the law of gravity, there is an ever-existing law that is constantly setting everything (seen and unseen) in motion. *The Law of Attraction* is the most powerful law in the Universe. It is basically the attractive, magnetic power of the Universe that draws similar energies together.

Many years ago, I played the guitar and bass guitar in a band in Mexico, and I discovered that by striking one string on my acoustic guitar, the same string on the other guitar would vibrate the same sound at the same time. It *was truly amazing! The energy of that specific sound would vibrate at the same frequency on the other guitar that was far away from me. This was the Law of* Attraction in action.

Just like the vibrational match to the sound of my guitar string, this law states that like attracts like at the level of thought, and that you will attract to yourself whatever you focus on, whatever you give your energy and attention to. You are a magnet! You will attract thoughts, ideas, people, situations, and circumstances into your life when you are a vibrational match to what you are focusing on.

This law is always in effect, it is always in motion, whether you understand it or not. Just like you may not understand how the human body works, even though you live in it. The body is a miracle that is always in motion, always creating itself, always healing itself, and everything is always working in perfect harmony.

Our bodies are a Spiritual manifestation of thought. Your current state of being is a manifestation of your own thought. Look at what we are made of, what exists beyond the cells in our bodies. The cells are made up of atoms, and the atoms are made of subatomic particles.

You find that the subatomic particles are nothing but Energy. This is where you find the truth. The truth is that we are beings of Energy, just as everything that exists. *Everything is Energy!* The stuff that the sun, the moon and the stars are made of, is the same stuff that we are made of.

Science has revealed that all matter is Energy, and Energy can never be created or destroyed. It is present everywhere all the time, it's always in motion, always moving from one form to another, and Energy changes form when we *shift* our *Awareness*, our *thoughts*, and our *vibration* about the things we are focusing on. This is how miracles of healing happen. This is how manifestation happens with everything that we focus our attention on. Energy always follows thought.

Our thoughts are Energy! They are cosmic magnetic waves that penetrate all time and space. Wow, this is how powerful we are! We are constantly creating our reality by virtue of what we think, whether we know it or not, whether we believe it or not, whether we understand it or not. So, whether you are creating positive thoughts or negative thoughts, whatever you are thinking is what you are attracting more of into your life. When you understand how the *Law of Attraction* works, you can begin to deliberately, consciously, and intentionally create your life!

> *Don't let life happen to you, Make life happen for you, NOW. -Magie Cook*

You are never surprised by what occurs in your experience if you truly understand this law, because you understand that the way you think has invited every circumstance into your life, and you know that you cannot manifest anything into your life experience without having invited that experience through your own thought.

> *The Law of Attraction allows for infinite possibilities, infinite abundance, and infinite joy. It knows no order of difficulty, and it can change your life in every way.*
> *–Jack Canfield*

This Universal Law is always in motion; it never takes a break. If you are running every day on auto pilot, then you are attracting the same average things you have always been attracting into your life. But if you make the choice to live each day in full *Awareness*, and apply the knowledge you now know, you will begin to see your own creative power in motion. You will begin to have so much fun with it, you will become an inspired Divine creator.

You create manifestation when you hold the image of what you want in your mind, when you *passionately focus* on it with *strong feeling* and *emotion*. You create manifestation, because when you focus on the thing you want most, you vibrate at the same frequency as the thing you are focusing on. This is how you bring it into your reality.

Your first step towards success begins when you make a decision to be *Aware* of what you are currently *thinking* and *feeling*, when you know how to apply the *vibration* of your current state of mind in relationship to what you want to attract into your reality.

If you are feeling good, you are vibrating at a high energy frequency. If you are feeling bad, you are vibrating at a low energy frequency. When you are focusing on a thought, you are controlling your vibration, and when you control your vibration, you control what you are attracting into your life. So, whatever it is that you want to attract to your life, all you have to do is see it, and hold that image in your mind with deep passionate emotion for as long as you can, and as often as you can. But this process must feel good, complete, and exhilarated. If it does not feel good, you are creating resistance, and when you create resistance you are attracting more of it. You must understand that the stronger the feelings and your emotions are, the stronger the power of attraction is. When you do this, you get into the same vibrational frequency of what you want. Only then, it begins to manifest in your reality, it is law. Everything that exists today, including the chair you are sitting in, the car you are driving, and the house you live in, was once a thought that manifested into physical form through someone else's imagination.

Our natural birthright is abundance, and you can never attract something into your life that you are not in harmony with. The problem that most of us have is that we are constantly thinking about what we don't want, and that is why the same problems keep manifesting into our lives. Did you know that research shows that the average person thinks 60,000 thoughts per day, and for most of us, 80% of our thoughts are negative self-talk?

The National Science Foundation published an

article in 2005 describing how the average person has about 12,000 to 60,000 thoughts per day. The article stated that 80% of the average person's thoughts are negative, and that 95% are exactly the same repetitive thoughts as the day before.

Another research conducted in 1985 by the University of Maryland School of Medicine showed how our internal and external dialogue significantly affects our hearts and blood pressure, and it alters the biochemistry of individual tissues in the farthest extremities of our bodies.

So now the question is, what happens when you are constantly thinking a negative thought? You are attracting the negative circumstances about that thought into your life. Remember that your thoughts are like magnets. So, if we are constantly thinking positive thoughts, we are attracting positive outcomes into our lives, but if we are constantly thinking negative thoughts, we are attracting negative outcomes into our lives. Let's stop for a minute here. Let's not be afraid, now that you know this truth. Let's not be overwhelmed into thinking that now you have to work hard at supervising all of your thoughts. Release that idea right now. Take a deep breath and let go!

The important thing to understand is that every thought has an attracting power, but some thoughts are more powerful in attraction than others. They have more power based on how much focus we put into them, based on how many feelings and emotions are attached to them. But here is the good news. Are you ready? Positive thoughts are far more powerful than negative thoughts, and whatever negative thoughts, bad feelings, or destructive beliefs you have had in the past, they can all be undone, and they can be cancelled!

It has been proven now scientifically that an affirmative thought is hundreds of times more powerful than a negative thought. –Michael Bernard Beckwith.

Here is more good news. The best way you can tell if you are having a powerful negative thought is through the *Awareness* of how you *feel*. Our feelings are the best feedback mechanism we have. You know that you are having a negative feeling (fear, guilt, anger, blame, resentment) because you feel it in your stomach, throat, or chest area. It is important to remember that *thoughts* with very *strong feelings* or *emotions* can become instant manifestations; this is true due to the fact that behind a *feeling* lies a *belief*, otherwise you wouldn't be having that feeling, and when you *believe* something to be *true*, it manifests, it becomes a miracle.

INSTANT MANIFESTATION

Growing up in the orphanage in Mexico, I taught myself how to ride horses and started riding bareback when I was 9 years old. I will always remember riding a horse that instantly took off running and bucking at the same time. It was so unexpected and so overpowering that, no matter how hard I pulled on his reins, he didn't respond. It was as if he had seen a ghost. He ended up throwing me off onto a big rock, where I landed on my stomach. I rolled over on the ground and stayed there for a few minutes to try to catch my breath. When I looked up, the horse just stood there right beside me, looking at me as if he was making fun of me. It almost looked like he had a smile on his face. When I was able, I firmly got up and looked him straight in the eyes as if I was challenging one of my brothers, and I said to the him, "Try to throw me off again!", and got right back up on him. After that incident, he never reacted or threw me on the ground again. Something amazing happened that day that I couldn't understand until later.

My horse "Nuevo"

Later one afternoon, when my brothers were trying to ride the horses in the field, the horses would do to them exactly the same thing they once did to me, over and over again. It was amazing to watch. I would get on the horses and race them back and forth with no problems right after they had bucked some of my brothers into the ground. So, they asked me, "Magie, how come the horses don't throw you off, but throw every one of us onto the ground?", and in that moment I discovered what was happening. I asked them, "When you are on the horse, are you afraid?" They said, "yes!" I said, "That is your problem. The moment that you choose not to be afraid, that's when they won't throw you off." Their problem was the result of instant manifestation on their fear-based thoughts and feelings. That day, I had the realization that animals can sense your emotional state of being and react to it instantly, just like a magnet. It was truly amazing! I later became a horse trainer and tamed all of the horses, mules, and donkeys we had.

I have experienced many instant manifestations in

my life based on strong emotional thoughts and feelings. The amazing experience for me was being aware in the moment and realizing what was happening.

When I purchased my first hard top convertible BMW, I drove it out of the dealership and got on the interstate. I had a sense of great joy knowing how I had manifested this great car through the Vision Board visualization process (you can read this story in Chapter 9). All of a sudden, I had this very powerful feeling that I was not worthy of this car. I had flashbacks and memories about living in poverty in an orphanage in Mexico, and I felt like I didn't deserve this car, that it was too much for me. As soon as I was having these strong emotional feelings, the tires of a semi-tractor trailer blew up in front of me and hit my car. It was such a sudden and powerful impact that it startled me into awareness. I realized what was happening and I started saying out loud, "I love this car, I deserve this car, I look awesome in it, it is perfect for me," and I just kept going on and on, and then I started laughing out loud! I pulled over and was very thankful that nothing happened to my car. This was the Universe's way of giving me constructive awareness. It was awesome!

The first step in self-mastery is to *remember who you really are.* You need to be in the present and living in the moment, to be *Aware* of what you are *thinking* and *feeling.* When you are having a negative thought-feeling, you must remember not to judge or punish yourself for it, you must remember to simply replace the "bad-feeling-thought" with a "good-or-better–feeling-thought", then another, and another, until there is no more room for that old limiting thought-feeling or belief in your reality.

THE ART OF ALLOWING

Another way to experience the power of manifestation is through *The Art of Allowing*. This is another powerful Universal Law. When you can clearly understand and remember *who you really are*, The Art of Allowing will become second nature to you. This is when you begin consciously guiding your thoughts in the direction of your desires. When you are allowing something to come into your life, you are open to the creative spiritual nature of the Universe. You say, "I open my entire being, my body, my spirit and my mind to you. I trust you." When you are practicing The Art of Allowing, you are trusting in your Higher Self. You are trusting in God, saying, "I know what I want, I don't know how I am going to achieve it, but I trust that everything I desire will come to me," and you feel very exhilarated during this process. When you are living in an allowing state, you feel and build on gratitude. You recognize all of the blessings you currently have, and you are thankful for everything that has already manifested into your life. You keep going with the flow, and you constantly feel good. You are grateful and thankful for the things you haven't manifested yet. The doors of your heart are wide open. You feel love, you are at peace, and you feel joy. This is where your real personal power lies!

Think about a river flowing downstream. You are flowing in it and everything that you want is also flowing within that river. Sooner or later, your desires catch up with you because you are magnetically attracting them by simply allowing them into your reality. You don't even have to swim or move a muscle; you are just going with the flow. Letting things flow into your experience, instead of creating contrast in the process of going after what you want, is the path of least resistance to manifestation, but you must trust and believe that you will receive what you are asking for.

When you are allowing, you are *Aware* of how you *feel*, and there are no doubts; there is no fear, only joy and a sense of peace, because you know that what you are asking is on its way. *(Refer to the story in Chapter 10 called Mindful Meditations™ where I manifested my greatest miracle through the art of allowing with the use of meditation).*

THERE ARE NO ACCIDENTS

Attracting undesired circumstances into your life simply means that you are off course, and that your thought process needs a *shift* in *Awareness*. But when you manifest something unwanted in your life, *it is perfect, because there are no accidents.* It is perfect because it creates Awareness that allows you to analyze your current emotional thought process and make the necessary changes to your current state of being. It is the Universe's way of giving you constructive Awareness. It allows you to grow. It allows you to become a stronger, wiser, and more powerful Spiritual Divine creator. It births in you new rockets of desire. It is perfect because you are choosing to see through the eyes of God, and when you choose to see good in everything, you attract greater things into your life. When something undesired happens in your life you can ask yourself, "How is this meant to make me better?" or, "What does this mean to teach me?"

Sometimes God takes the things you hold most dear in life for very important reasons; perhaps it is preparing you for something greater, and perhaps there is something you must learn in order to grow, something that allows you to create a much more enlightened path to your true happiness. Being homeless was the best experience and the best gift I received (you can read the full story in Chapter 5 called Got Faith?). The situation allowed me to re-evaluate my entire self, to be reborn, and to see everything with new eyes. I came out with a new vision, and I acquired much more success than before. The greatest enlightenment I have received as a result of these experiences was the realization that even if I didn't have ANYTHING at all (money, cars, a business, a home, or a relationship), I could achieve even greater happiness, and completely love myself unconditionally, because all I needed was "Me," and God's Spirit within me. I had the realization that having nothing at all felt even better for me. I was peaceful, I had nothing to worry about, there were no problems, and I was complete.

Right when I graduated high school, I got recruited to play basketball for the Mexican National Team in Mexico City. My father and I had waited three months to get a call back from them. The orphanage where we lived had big open fields everywhere, and one day my brothers and I went out to play football. My brother Julio was throwing very long passes, and a bunch of us at the other end were competing to see who could catch most of the throws. Julio threw a very long pass towards me, which I caught very nicely, but awkwardly fell into the ground, shoulder first. I broke my collarbone!

I immediately went to see my father, and with deep emotion, he grabbed me by the shoulders and told me, "Your dreams are over!" I was devastated! I cried a little, but I KNEW that something better was going to happen for me! In that moment, I chose not to believe his words. I chose not to let them impact me for one second!

Three days later, the Mexican National Team called us, and it felt even more devastating, but I believed and trusted that something better was coming my way. I didn't know what was coming my way, but I just believed.

In the midst of this chaos, I was at peace with myself, and I didn't worry. I didn't worry about what was going to happen next. I simply let the perfect circumstances flow into my life. I was practicing The Art of Allowing and didn't even know it. I didn't know what my future was going to be like, and I didn't know what direction I was going into. I was letting God's blessings flow into my life, and they did!

When I got recruited to play basketball for the Mexican National Team in Mexico City

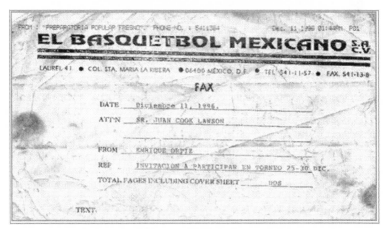

Recruitment letter from the Mexican National Team

Often times in our lives when we go without, when we lose the most precious things that we value and hold, fear strikes, and we immediately worry about how we will manage. Worrying is resisting to what you truly want. Worry has fear attached all over your thoughts, and when you have fear attached to your thoughts, you attract more of the things that you are having fears about. Even when you say, "I really, really want, or I really, really need..." you are creating resistance to that which you want to obtain. You worry because you feel discomfort, because you feel lack, because you think you can't do without. The truth is, you should simply go within and ask, declare it, and release it, and trust that God will manifest that which you want in due time. Let everything good flow your way. Believe that you can have what you are asking for, believe that you deserve what you are asking for, and be ready to receive with open arms.

Four months later, my parents took a bus and 68 of my adopted and biological siblings, and traveled the United States looking for support for my parents' non-profit organization for the poor. In order for all of us to fit in the bus, my father took half of the seats out of the bus so the rest of us could sit on the floor towards the back of the bus. While in the States, we were invited to stop by and have a picnic at a school in Charleston, West Virginia.

When we arrived, the first thing I saw was a basketball court. My brothers and I immediately ran towards it, grabbed a basketball and started to play. At the picnic happened to be the Women's Head Coach of the University of Charleston. She saw me play and asked some people around, "Who is that girl?" She went to look for my father and told him, "I want her to come play for me on a scholarship!"

My team at the University of Charleston; from left to right, I am the third person on the bottom left, on one knee

My *belief* and *allowing* that something better was coming my way became a reality. *The Law of Attraction* and *The Art of Allowing* were indeed in action, and everything worked in my favor.

If you choose to believe that there are no accidents,

then you will open the doors for abundance, even if you don't know what is coming, because you are always expecting something better. There is always purpose and a reason behind every event; the question is, are we aware enough to discover what the seed of opportunity is?

3
Not Only Thoughts Become Things

Success is a state of mind. You have the truly amazing ability to create endless and magical possibilities, and unlimited abundance in this journey. You also have the ability to neglect and destroy every opportunity that comes your way. Your mentality is everything. Success is all about the way you consciously use your mind; it's about the way you think, that you can create your reality.

You must understand that you are fully responsible for your happiness; no one else is, and no one else can be. If you depend on someone else to be responsible for your happiness, you will experience constant disappointment. You are responsible for your happiness because you truly love yourself, because you want to experience joy, unconditional love, inner peace, and all of the goodness that life brings in your favor. You are a powerful Spiritual Divine creator fully in control of your destiny.

CHOOSING HAPPINESS

My life has been a tremendous journey. I made a decision in my early childhood to stay happy, and to have a positive state of mind, no matter what came my way. I always said to myself that I could turn every "feel bad" situation into a "feel good" one, and I did! This was a gift. I experienced many difficult things in my childhood, including poverty. Living in an orphanage, with sometimes more than 200 children at a time, was very challenging. Some days were better, and some were worse. There was a lot of neglect, and in some cases, abuse. I saw a lot of fear and suffering in all of the kids that came in. Every single one of them had their own traumas and suffering, from their own previous homes or from living on the streets.

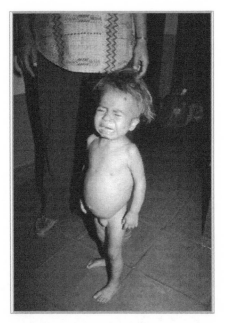

Rosita became one of my adoptive sisters. She was severely malnourished when she arrived.

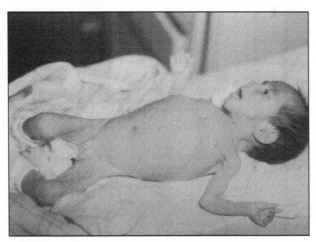

Esperanza was another adopted sister who was in critical condition with only one week to live when she arrived.

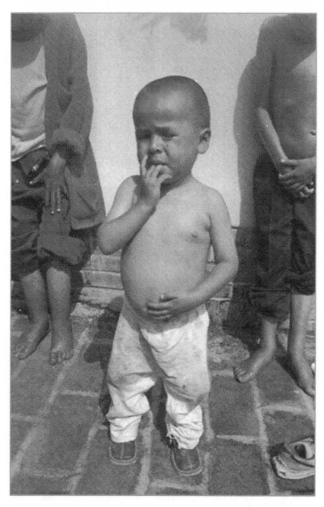

Joel was another one of my adoptive siblings that came in severely malnourished. He is now a veterinarian and takes care of the animals at the orphanage.

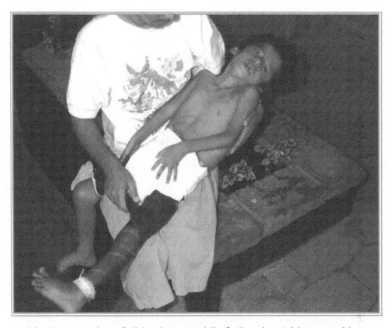

Mario came in a full body cast. His father beat him up with a baseball bat and broke almost every bone in his body. His head, face and mouth were deformed because of the abuse he received. He was so afraid of everyone that he would panic and cry if anyone walked into the room he was in.

*Both Teresita and Angelica were sexually abused
victims in their previous families.*

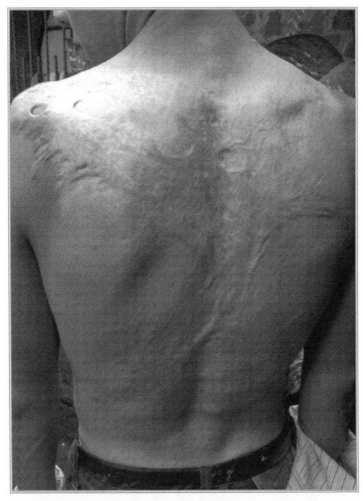

Carlito's' father burned him with a fire torch all over his body and stabbed him in the stomach. Both he and his brother Christian could not speak when they first arrived. My parents thought they were mentally challenged, but one month later they started developing speech. My parents later found out that their parents had kept them in a locked room all of their lives, only shoving food underneath the door to keep them alive.

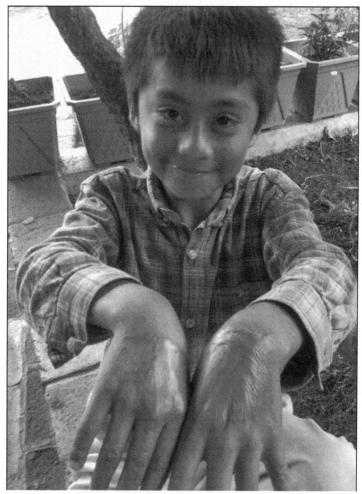

*Miguel and his sister were both burned by their
mother with an iron for punishment.*

Moses was abandoned at our gate because his mother didn't want him anymore. I still remember hearing the doorbell ring and the bus taking off when my father and I walked down to the gate and saw him sitting there. My father named him Moses based on the story in the Bible.

These are just a few of the stories of some of my adoptive siblings. Every one of them came in with a traumatic past, and every one of them has a story.

Living in the orphanage, I was blessed with the gift of being able to discern between the good and bad things I saw and learn from other people's mistakes. There, I learned the difference between what I wanted and didn't want in my future life as an adult. Instead of being overwhelmed with everyone's problems, I chose to become a dreamer. I used my mind to create my life adventures. I became a soldier, Rambo, The Karate Kid, Superman, Rocky, an Indian, a cowboy, a horse trainer, a hunter, Michael Jordan, and many other characters. I was always in my own little world, disappearing into the mountains for long periods of time without anyone noticing. I literally created my own toys, like my weapons, my bows and arrows, my slingshots, and my guns, made out of wood carved out with my knives. I made little houses made of cardboard, where I would sleep when we didn't have beds. I would even dig caves with my knives in steep canyons (canyons that you could barely walk on with over 100 yards of steep drops) as my secret hiding places, where I would sleep and sometimes just hide my stuff. I would carve holes in the walls of my caves and hide my food or knives in them, then patch them with mud with a big X on them so I would know where my stuff was. I began hiding my food like that because, during the night, the wild animals would eat my food.

I was free. My goal was to always feel good no matter what the circumstances were. I had a gift. I had my mind. I became a dreamer. I was a Superhero, and I was invincible.

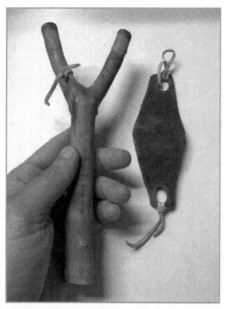

I carved this slingshot with my knife, and my father took it away because I killed a bird with it. He gave it back to me many years later.

This is one of the cardboard houses I built. While everyone else slept on the floor, I made this my little adventurous home.

This was the biggest cave I dug. It was my secret hiding place in the canyon. This cave ended up being about fifteen feet deep and four feet tall.

These are some of the adventures that I relived with my family. From left to right: Jonatan, Manuel, Moses, Custodio, Josue and Jose.

The first step on the path of achieving success is to take complete responsibility for your actions; that is, to take full responsibility of the way you think, to know and understand that within your mind lays limitless power for unleashing your success.

One simple thought has a very powerful energetic and magnetic force. It is a force that becomes a manifestation, if that thought becomes the focus of your desire. In his book, *The Key to Living the Law of Attraction*, Jack Canfield talks about how your thoughts are not just wispy little clouds drifting through your head, and that your thoughts are things. They are actually measurable units of energy; they are biochemical electrical impulses. They are waves of energy that, as far as we can tell, penetrate all time and space.

But I am here today to tell you that not only thoughts become things. Your thoughts are the inception of an idea, they are the driving force to every manifestation, but they can only become intensely magnified in power when you have *feelings* attached to them, when your *emotions* play a role in the thought process. Your emotions are internal passionate energies that manifest the feeling as if you are already there. This is the feeling of experiencing what you want "Now," in this moment. You either feel really good or you feel very bad, based on what you are thinking. You can either feel love, joy, peace, happiness, and gratitude, or you feel fear, guilt, shame, and so on. A positive emotion (love) and a negative emotion (fear) cannot co-exist at the same time in your body.

Your natural birthright is abundance, and when you feel something positive with deep passionate emotion, you are inviting the reality of that natural place where you want to be. You feel like you are already there, because that is what it feels like when you are already there, within your current manifestation. When you think something into being with emotions attached to them, you also create a visualization within your internal experience, and you don't even realize you are doing this. And now that you have created an internal visualization of it, you have created a picture, an image in your Subconscious mind, and because your Subconscious mind cannot tell the difference between reality or an imagined thought or image, this image is now a memory that will materialize in your reality, and it is now just a matter of time.

Nothing that exists today came to be without a thought process behind it, whether that thought is positive or negative.

It is in the way that you *think*, the way that you *feel*, and *also* the way that you *choose to see* the world that creates your reality. You have a choice! You have the option of looking at things as they are, or you have the option of imagining them as you want them to be. You have the choice to *see* and *believe* that everything is difficult or easy, to think and believe that you are weak or strong, healthy or sick. Whatever side you choose, your mind will produce a vibration within you that will equal your point of attraction. When this happens, the events and circumstances that match the vibrations that you are putting out will line up for you. For example, if you see suffering, then you will see more suffering, but if you see love, then you will see more love. What you choose to see is what you get.

SEEING INTO BEING

One afternoon, my team and I at Maggie's Salsa had finished a very long day of producing our products for one of our largest supermarket chains. The refrigerated truck was fully packed and ready to go, but there was one problem! My driver didn't show up to take the delivery. I had worked a very long day with only a few hours of sleep the night before. Even though the destination was about eight hours away, I decided to jump into the truck and take the delivery myself. When I jumped into the truck, I encountered another problem! The refrigeration unit would not turn on. I said to myself, "Oh no! What am I going to do?" In trying to think quickly because it was already 5:00 pm that afternoon, I took my smartphone and Googled, "truck refrigeration repair places nearby". I found one place and called them immediately. I said to the guy on the other end of the line, "I know you don't know me, but I have a truck full of product and my refrigeration unit is not working. I have an eight-hour drive and I must deliver these products; will you please stay open for me to come in so you can fix my unit?"

He was a little hesitant but agreed to wait for me. According to my smartphone, the truck refrigeration repair place was about 30 minutes away. So, I jumped into the truck and started to drive towards the direction of the shop. On my way there, I felt this amazing sensation overcome my entire being. I began to shed a few tears. I had the thought that I could be driving back to the manufacturing plant not being able to take this delivery. In that moment, I decided to shift the way that I was thinking! Even though both of my hands were gripping the steering wheel, I visualized both of my arms wide open and started saying to myself, "Victory! Victory! I made it!" I saw myself successfully driving the load to my final destination.

When I got there, I parked the truck inside the shop, and I met this guy for the first time. He grabbed a ladder and climbed to the top of the refrigeration unit. The whole time he was looking at it, he was shaking his head, and I could see the bad expression on his face. I sat down by the curbside and I just closed my eyes, believing that he would be able to fix it. About thirty minutes later, I heard the unit turn on! I opened my eyes and looked at him at the top of the unit. He had a half smile on his face, but he also had a look of disbelief in the fact that whatever he did to repair it had worked. He said, "Well., it's good to go!" I jumped up in excitement and told him, "Do you realize what you just did? Do you realize how much product I have in the back of that truck?", and he just kept smiling at me. I had over $20,000 worth of products in the back of that truck that required refrigeration.

I went to get my checkbook, and when I opened it up, I only had one check left. I told the guy, "Look, isn't this amazing?" He just wouldn't stop smiling at me. I drove my products that afternoon successfully to their final destination on time. On my way there, I was completely exhilarated and overjoyed at what I had created by believing and seeing myself as manifested success.

If you change the way you look at things, the things you look at change. -Dr. Wayne Dyer

Often, we go through our lives offering a thought based on what we see. One example is when we are so quick to judge people, even before meeting them. I have found it to be very inspiring that when I begin to judge someone I first meet, I imagine their bodies evaporate, and all I see is their light, shining across to mine. I acknowledge that I am beginning to interact with a beautiful Divine being. I am connected to them in Spirit and it feels so exhilarating!

Because most of us go through our lives offering a thought based on what we have seen and experienced in our past, we create this lie based on those illusions, and because we can see things with our own eyes, we can touch them with our hands, we can smell it with our senses, we let the circumstances around us determine our current moods, vibrations, and the way we feel. We forget that what we see in this reality is just an illusion, and sometimes what we see changes us forever. Sometimes what we see stays deeply rooted within our Subconscious mind. These events are later triggered by a random experience and appear in our lives in the form of energy blocks, preventing us from experiencing the joyful life we want to live. When we are in Spirit, we are no longer affected by the things that we see; instead, we see love in everything because we understand what things really are, and we understand who people really are; they are One in Spirit, just like us. We begin to see with the eyes of God, in their perfect nature.

A perfect example of this understanding is the miracle-performing life of Jesus. When He healed the sick, he never saw them as sick, he always saw them as perfectly healthy. When he asked them, "Do you believe you can be healed?" they replied, "YES", and the miracle happened immediately. He was a very wise man who was in connection with the power of God (All that is), and, being tuned into his Higher Self, used the power of Mind to not only see them as healthy, but influenced them into seeing themselves as healthy. He had the power to get into the same level of Mind, in the same mentality, in the same nature of the sick person reaching for that thought that made them sick, and change that thought, creating an instant miracle manifestation in their lives. He planted a seed of belief. This is how his miracles worked. His influence was magical!

Unfortunately, when we came into this world, we

were born into a world of fear and doubt. As children, we enjoyed playing, discovering, exploring, and growing in the purest essence, but for some of us, somewhere along the road, everything stopped. We lived pure in essence, but because we were constantly surrounded by our negative environment, passed down to us by our friends, our teachers, and our loved ones, we became prisoners of our own minds, prisoners of fear, doubt, anger, jealousy, and shame. We became victims of a crippled mentality. We were domesticated to think this way.

When we constantly surround ourselves with negative circumstances and people, some of us tend to become like them. Just like the baby who is born into a neighborhood of crime and drugs, when he is a young boy, at first, he is afraid, and he resists the circumstances around him. The years go by, and he no longer is afraid or resistant because he has gotten used to his environment. When he becomes a teenager, he is so comfortable with his environment that he becomes the drug trafficker, the perpetrator of violence, and this is the only way he knows how to live, how to survive. This is his life. For him, there is no other way.

THE BEGGAR

One Thursday afternoon, I accompanied my father to the city of Morelia in Mexico. As we were walking to the bank to cash his checks he had received in the mail, my father was filled with compassion when he saw a homeless young man with no legs begging for money on the side of a heavy traffic road. My father approached him and gently told the man, "I am a doctor, I can give you legs, and you will be able to walk again!" The young man got angry with him and said, "Go away! My mother said this is the best way I can make money!" This young man was conditioned to think that this was the best life he could ever get. He was limited by what he thought, and he was limited by what was passed down to him. My father walked away in disbelief feeling rejected for trying to help someone in suffering.

Who you are today is just a reflection of what you have been in the past; and whatever beliefs you have bought or sold from the people around you, whatever spiritual bondages you carry, they can be undone, by understanding the real nature of *who you really are*, and connecting to God, seeking guidance to break away from what is keeping you in suffering.

MAGIE COOK

4

The Mind

The Mind is the moving force of your current manifestations. The Mind is the connection to "All That Is", and it is infinite in nature. The *Infinite Mind* is all knowing and is the infinite supply of all intelligence. The Mind is the unity of Spirit, Soul, and Body, the unity of cause, medium, and effect, the unity of Father, Son, and Holy Ghost. If you are seeking a shift from your current reality, a transformational experience, you must know and understand how The Mind works, and how you can turn this knowledge into your own success.

The truth is that your life is a physical manifestation

of what goes on in your subjective mind. The subjective mind is our identity in Infinite Mind. It is the result of our mental attitudes. This is where we house all of the images, suggestions, impressions, and inherited tendencies, as far as we want to believe and accept them.

The Mind is made of two very important parts: The **Conscious mind**, which is the Spirit within you, and the **Subconscious mind**, which is your Soul.

-Your Conscious mind is that power of consciousness that knows itself. It is the reasoning mind. It is conscious of its own being.

-The Subconscious mind is like the soil in the ground where the creation sprouts. It receives whatever information is given from the Conscious mind and simply acts. It does not know, like the Conscious mind knows, but it is the one who carries out the will of the Conscious mind. It does not know right from wrong, or good from bad, it simply acts as commanded and manifests. With this fact, we can say that to believe in the way your mind works is to believe in belief itself.

> *"I am no longer cursed by poverty because I took possession of my own mind, and that mind has yielded me every material thing I want, and much more than I need. But this power of mind is a universal one, available to the humblest person as it is to the greatest"*
> *— Andrew Carnegie.*

One of the most important gifts that we could give ourselves is the gift of *thoughtful awareness*. We must be *impeccable with our words*. You can certainly tell what someone is thinking by their choice of words they speak. Have you ever heard someone say, "It breaks my heart," or "It's so sick," over and over again? Think about what they are telling their bodies; think about what they are manifesting into their lives.

When I was in the process of creating a water product for my new business, I came across a research scientist named Dr. Masaru Emoto. In his many years of research, he discovered how human consciousness, (the energy and vibrations of thoughts and words) have a tremendous effect on the molecular structure of water, simply by giving intent to it. In his research, you can see how frozen water crystals respond to words with positive intent versus words with negative intent. The use of certain words literally changes the appearance of the crystals, from dull and ugly to bright and beautiful magnificent designs. It is truly incredible to see this phenomenon. Now, think about this: if change happens to water crystals simply by giving intent to them, think about what happens to our bodies. Our bodies are made of 75 to 90% water!

Here is another awareness factor we need to know of. When you tell someone, "Don't slam the door!", guess what the Subconscious hears? "Slam the Door." When you tell someone, "Don't wreck my car!", the Subconscious hears, "Wreck my car!" When you say, "I am not stupid", the Subconscious hears, "I am stupid." When you are saying these things, you are magnifying the attracting power of these words because you are expressing your deep emotions about how you feel. The truth is that your Subconscious mind does not see things in words, it sees everything in pictures. It does not see "don't, or not". So instead of saying, "Don't slam the door", you can say, "Please close the door gently", and instead of saying, "Don't wreck my car", you can say, "Drive safely".

DON'T TOUCH!

This awareness helped me remember a dramatic incident I never forgot from when I was very young. My mother had sat me down on her mosaic kitchen counter as she was making her famous and delicious flour tortillas one morning. I clearly remember her pointing at the outlet nearby and saying the words, "Don't touch!" (no tocar) I don't know what came over me, but I had the strong urge to stretch out my arm and put my finger into the outlet. I was not being rebellious at all. She gave me the command, "Don't touch!", but my Subconscious mind heard, "Touch!" (tocar). I touched, and I got the worse shocking pain I had ever experienced. My mother said to me, "I told you... Don't touch!" It must have been very confusing for me at the time. What a tremendous realization this knowledge is. We must be aware of what we constantly say, let go of the old hidden harmful sayings, and create new habits to stay impeccable with our words. It truly impacts our reality and the reality of those around us!

It is very important for parents to be aware of this knowledge in choosing their words with their children, because children tend to be more connected to their Higher Self than adults in the purest sense, and so what you command them to do they will obey with no questions asked, because they trust you.

FEELINGS IN WORDS

We must also be *Aware* of the *feelings* that are attached to our *words*. When we say, "I never want to experience a divorce," or, "I will never get breast cancer," you are creating exactly what you don't want, but with more power. More power, because you now have *strong feelings* attached to your *words*, which were once your thoughts. If you take the word "never" out of the expressions above, what does your Subconscious hear? Exactly! Not only are you using the word "never", but you are also attaching fear to that thought, and when you attach fear to your thought, guess what happens? It manifests.

I will always remember an incident that occurred while I was living in the orphanage in Mexico. A beautiful young girl showed up to my Father's clinic one Sunday afternoon. She was covered with warts from head to toe. I watched my dad burn each and every one of them with an electrical gun. It took him two days to finish the procedure. She was very brave. She didn't cry at all, but she would cringe and make noises with her mouth every time the electrical gun would zap her. I clearly remember the unpleasantness of the room, including the smell of the procedure. The smell was so strong that my father had to take the procedure outside. I was so impacted by what I saw that I said to myself, "I am never going to have warts". I was so certain of it, but what I didn't realize was that I had attached a tremendous amount of fear to that incident. I was deeply traumatized by that event and I was sure it was not going to happen to me. Several months later, guess what happened? I got warts on my hands! My father had to do the same procedure on me that he did with that young girl. The scars on my hands are now a constant reminder of this reality!

Everything that we say to ourselves or others, every suggestion is planted in the Subconscious mind and become memories that eventually externalize in the body, so we must be *Aware* of what we are telling ourselves! Every spoken word will always have a great impact on the ears that hear. A *word* is the process in which *beliefs* are formed and *manifestation* created.

In the beginning was the Word, and the Word was with God, and the Word was God. John 1:1

The Word is the creator of the entire Universe and everything else in it. Your word is the creating factor of your life, and your thoughts become your deeply rooted beliefs that were once words. The Word is the ability of the Spirit to declare itself into manifestation, into form.

You must be impeccable with your word!

When you see someone speaking mostly about illness, they are sick, but when you see someone speaking of prosperity, they have it. When you see someone speaking about love, they are love! You must pay attention to the words you speak. Your words are meant to uplift and inspire yourself and others, and that is your true nature. Your words are influential, so be impeccable with your word!

INFLUENCE

When I lived in the orphanage, I learned a very important lesson that gave me a tremendous amount of compassion, and it changed my life forever. In watching all of the suffering around me, I learned that physical punishment and abuse did nothing but create a tremendous amount of fear. You were constantly afraid of getting in trouble, and because you were afraid, you attracted trouble even if you didn't do anything wrong at all. Because of my childhood experiences, I have images in my mind of severe punishment that I will always remember. They are constant reminders of how different I will be with my kids someday. These experiences were very agonizing for me, but one day I did something that changed me! One of my adoptive brothers, Luis, came to me crying, he said, "Magie, Anabel bit me". Luis was about 5 years old at the time, and Anabel was around the same age as well. I told Luis, "Tell Anabel to come here". When they both came into my presence, I asked Anabel why she had bit Luis. She said, "He was bothering me!" Then I asked both of them, "What do you think I am going to do now?" They both said, "You are going to tell Mom". I asked, "And what is Mom going to do?" They said, "She is going to punish us", and then I asked again, "And what is Mom going to do after that?" They replied, "She is going to tell Dad", then I asked once again, "And what is Dad going to do?" They again replied, "He is going to punish us again"! At this time, they had started to cry. I firmly looked into their eyes and said to them, "I am not going to do that!" They looked at me with a very surprised look on their faces. What I did that day was just to sit down for 15 minutes and talk to both of them. When I had finished my conversation, I got up and started walking towards the door. When I was almost at the door, I had a strong urge to stop and look back. In that moment, I saw both of them embracing each other with tears in their eyes. I could see their compassion for each other. I was so deeply moved that I started to cry as well. I said to myself, "That is how I want to be with my kids!" I also wished that my parents had done that with us, but there were just so many of us. After this happened, I had the Spiritual realization of how powerful words are. I started doing this with all of my siblings and received a lot of respect and love from them in return. They listened to me, they admired me, and they felt safe with me.

From left to right: Teresita, Anabel and Luis

One Saturday afternoon, most of my siblings were gathered playing soccer in the basketball court at the orphanage. There must have been 5 different teams of all ages, waiting to play whoever the losers were from the game that was currently in session. It was almost time for dinner and my oldest biological sister started to yell, "A comer!" (Which means, "Time for dinner"). She stood there yelling for a long time, the same thing over and over again. I was surprised and mesmerized to see that no one was paying attention to her. She was about to give up when she saw me looking at her. She yelled across the court with a desperate voice, "Magie, no one is paying attention to me!" At that moment, I stood up, whistled, and said, "Kids, dinner time!" They all stopped, looked at me, and all ran directly to the dining room. My sister's jaw dropped! She said, "How did you do that?" I just looked at her and smiled. They respected and loved me so much, and I had great influence over them because I loved and respected them too, and when I spoke, they listened to me. That was truly amazing!

My team after playing mud soccer one evening

To know how to use your Mind and apply it to anything you desire equals success, in EVERY area of your life. One of my favorite prayers was written by Napoleon Hill and it goes like this:

"Oh Divine providence, I ask not for more riches, but more wisdom, for which to accept and use wisely, the riches you have given me at birth, in the form of the power to control and direct my mind to whatever ends I desire".

He understood the power of using The Mind, the power of Intention to create ANYTHING he desired.

God asked King Solomon if there was anything he wanted, and said he could ask for it and God would give it to him, King Solomon asked for WISDOM. God said to him, "If you would have asked for riches, I would have given them to you, but of all things, I give you wisdom". Solomon understood the value of wisdom of The Mind. He understood that wisdom is the creator and builder of EVERYTHNG he wanted, and Solomon became the most wealthy, rich, and prosperous man on earth of his time. With all of his wisdom, he gave God all the glory for all of his manifestations.

The greatest wisdom to have of is to remember *who we really are*, and to know that we have access to ALL POWER as amazing Divine Spiritual beings, and that this GREATER POWER does not solely come from us, but the power of God through us.

5

Got Faith?

Faith in success is a state of mind, a state in which you *believe* that you are already successful. The secret to success in every area of your life happens when you come to *believe* in yourself, when you have complete *Faith* in yourself. When you truly *believe* something to be true for you, *it is done*. When you truly *believe* something to be true, you are *One* in relationship with your Subconscious mind, and you will automatically manifest your reality.

When you understand how *The Mind* works *(refer to the Chapter 4, to read about The Mind)*, you will know

Faith, you will *believe* in the way that your mind works. You will *believe* in manifestation from the unseen when you come to understand how the *Law of Attraction* works *(refer to Chapter 2 to read about The Universal Law)*, how *Cause, Medium, and Effect work.* You will consciously know how to use your power to manifest what you desire.

I have an adoptive brother who had an old white truck, and when it didn't start, he believed that by tapping a certain part in the engine three times with a pipe (not one or two times) it would start, and it did, every single time! I just smiled at him because I understood how he was doing it.

When our fork truck at our manufacturing plant would suddenly die on us, my business partner would call me down from the office and tell me, "Magie, get on the fork truck, it always turns on when you get on it," and it did. She believed that I had the power to make it start because every time the fork truck wouldn't work, I would tell her, "Every time I get on it, it turns on. I have a special touch, it's my energy", and she was always amazed at this. I can still remember the look on her face with her wide-open eyes and her body language; it was as if she was expressing, "See, it always turns on when you get on it". It is amazing how the power of creation and miracles are in motion by the tremendous power of our beliefs.

All throughout my life, I have always believed that when something traumatic or bad happens to me, there is always the seed of something better. Traumatic events have taught me that there is always something to learn from them. I have always believed that there are no accidents, and my so-called accidents are always perfect in all nature, perfect for me because they have allowed me to grow and expand into what makes me a stronger and better person. I have always believed that everything always happens for a reason and with a purpose, I just had to discover what those reasons were, and I did by living in the moment, by being Aware.

Wouldn't it be wonderful if we would all start to believe that, no matter what life brings us, everything would work for the greatest good for us? That we will continue to receive unlimited abundance, inexhaustible joy, and unmeasured happiness? Those are wonderful beliefs to have, but the truth is that most of us are constantly guided by our limiting beliefs, not being Aware that we have them, not knowing how to shift them, and we keep attracting undesired effects or results into our lives.

At the end of tax season in 2010, all of my team members in my company received their tax return checks from the IRS. I could see the excitement on everyone's faces for having the extra cash. One of my team members, who is 44 years old, approached me and said, "Look Magie, I just got a check for $1,100 from the IRS. I am rich! I am not coming back to work". I got deeply saddened by this and his poor financial set point. I knew that he would be here asking for his job back soon. Sure enough, he was back the following week. He had spent all of his money, every penny of it.

In order to truly break away from our limiting beliefs and negative patterns, in order to truly release the shackles that keep us attracting the same undesired results into our lives, we must become *Aware* in our experience, and we must quiet our minds, we must go within and find out what those negative beliefs are!

You can begin to ask questions like,

-Why am I attracting poverty in my life?

-What are my beliefs about money?

-What are the patterns I go through when I lose my money?

If you feel discomfort when asking these questions,

ask where the discomfort is coming from.

-*Was it something your parents always said?*

-*Was it something you saw?*

-*Was it something that happened to you?*

When you discover what the source of our limiting beliefs is, you will find that a lot of these limiting beliefs were kind of silly to begin with, and through your power of Awareness you can begin to release them, and you can begin to shift them.

Yes, you can build on your Faith and shift your negative beliefs by flooding your subconscious mind with positive life-altering affirmations through the use of Autosuggestion, and you can also make it a habit to be Aware of the words you speak. For example, let's say that you decided to create an affirmation today that says,

-*Money flows to me in abundance.*

When you say this to yourself at first, your Conscious mind will probably say, "yeah, right", but let me tell you what happens when you repeat an affirmation every single day, when you affirm to yourself what you truly want. What happens is that your Subconscious mind starts to *believe* what your Conscious mind is saying, and once the message is *enveloped* and *believed* by the Subconscious mind, *it must manifest, it is law.* But you will not experience true success or quicker results until you truly discover what is holding you back, especially within your *deeply rooted beliefs.*

Only you hold the key to unleashing your success, and when you choose to shift your beliefs through your Awareness, you will begin to create positive changes in your life.

Throughout our lives, we create our beliefs based on many different circumstances, one being based on what our loved ones said because we view them as experts, we look up to them, we respect and admire who they are. We create our beliefs based on what we see or hear on the television, we create our beliefs based on what we hear from our friends, or people who we consider to be experts in any field.

Every time I watch the Dr. Oz show, I am truly amazed at how much impact the show has on its viewers. I see constant shifts in beliefs in people. What they once thought was true all of the sudden is a myth, and their lives are changed. Their lives change because they see things, circumstances and events as impacting their happiness and wellbeing. It is truly amazing to watch this show. Once you create a belief, you are bonded to it; no can tell you that you are wrong about that belief, unless there is much higher perceived proof that debunks the current belief you hold.

If you believe that cancer is a hereditary trait and that you will get breast cancer because both your mother and your grandmother had it, then you are more likely to attract having breast cancer in your lifetime. But the truth is, this fear-based belief is just an illusion based on what you perceive to be real. Fear does not exist but is only in your Mind. It is simply a negative belief that you bought from the people around you, or from something that you saw that eventually manifested in your body. Even if diseases seem to be hereditary, the spiritual bondage that you have with this perception can be undone *(refer to Chapter 13 called Suffering & Releasing your Breaks, to learn about hereditary spiritual bondage, and how to break the patterns that are keeping you in suffering).*

Your body was designed to heal itself, and it does so automatically all the time; it is the natural way to be, the natural way of being healthy and abundant. What keeps us sick are our negative patterns and beliefs about what we are not. It is a lie that we have manufactured within our beautiful being, a lie that can be reversed, a belief that can be shifted, and a Spiritual bondage that can be broken.

So, what happens when we choose to believe in something unseen, something that has not been manifested in physical form yet? Only when we understand how The Mind works, will we be able to move freely to creating our deepest desires. Knowing how The Mind works is having Faith in the creative nature of "All that Is" which exists within us, an Awareness that will ultimately deliver to you all of your gifts. Here is where the creative process begins, where all of the magic unfolds. This is so much fun, because you get to manifest untold blessings and surprises, along with the things we are asking for. It's like you are receiving abundant gifts from the Universe, and some of them are unexpected.

Inspired Action or simply acting on what you want to

manifest is having Faith; it's believing in yourself; it's believing in your future manifestations. Before I started writing this book, I decided to hire a photographer. I took my cover photos and designed my cover page. I also told everyone I knew about my book. I printed my cover photo on paper and cut it to fit a book I had in my library. Every time I sat down on my desk, the first thing I saw was my book, and I visualized people having tremendous joy reading it. I have never written a book before, but doing these simple things gave me the faith that I could make this happen for me. During this process, I attracted a wonderful marketing company to market my book, and many other wonderful gifts and surpluses that came along with my ultimate manifestation. I have used this method to manifest many gifts to my life throughout my journey! (refer to Chapter 7, called Inspired Action, to read more stories like this).

I am going to share with you an amazing story about the Faith of a little boy. The story tells of a small village that was suffering from a severe drought. Everything was dying: the crops, the animals, and the villagers had started to suffer from the effects as well. To try to find the solution, the village priest called the villagers to gather at the village square to pray for rain. He told everyone to bring a token of their faith so that the prayer would be done in sincere faith. When everyone showed up, so did a nine-year-old boy with an open umbrella. Sure enough, within a few moments it began to rain. Wow! What an act for believing!

It is true that some miracles happen much faster than others, but this all depends on the nature of your belief, on the nature of your Faith in what you want. There is no time limit for the Universe, for God, there is no such thing as too big or too small, it just manifests according to the extent in which you believe.

Faith is knowing that whatever you are asking for is already there.

The Subconscious mind does not care if you are asking for $50,000 or $500,000, the time frame for its manifestation depends solely upon you, it depends on what you believe. If you believe that it will take five years to earn $500,000, then it will take five years for you. When I write my goals, my affirmations, and vision boards, I don't limit myself in possibilities, I simply write what I want, and I print or create visual photos of what I want to have. I never worry about the "hows" because I understand the Spiritual power of Mind, and how it works. At 33 years old, I have seen proof of this in all of the miracles and successes I have manifested in my life.

> *Therefore, I tell you, whatever you ask for in prayer,*
> *believe that you have received it, and it will be yours.*
> *Mark 11:12*

To make Faith part of your success is to have the understanding that *Faith* (your belief) in the *unseen* (what you want, but we don't currently have proof that it exists) is what will manifest your desire, by the *belief* and understanding of how *The Mind* works. You will begin to understand this concept only when you start applying the knowledge and success principles from this book into your life. You will truly believe when you begin manifesting your own miracles. Things that you initially thought were impossible for you to attain, will come true for you, but it is only when you start to shift the way you think.

LIVING BY FAITH

My father once asked me to travel with him to the city of Morelia in Mexico one Thursday. One the way, he picked up all of his patients that he had given medical *consultations the prior Sunday. He was taking his patients to the Hospital Civil in Morelia to see a specialized doctor for their surgeries. Thursdays were always full of excitement for my father. It was when he received a package full of mail containing checks from US donors for the Mano De Ayuda program for the poor. His face was full of light, and he had a bright smile! "No more struggling this week," he said. We had received $1,000 in the mail. As we were sitting in his van in the parking lot of the hospital, an old man started to approach us. My father said to me, "Do you know how I can tell that this man is very poor and malnourished?" I said, "No, how?" He said, "Look at his feet. He has no shoes; and look at his hair, it is very fine and discolored." The man approached us and asked to speak with my father privately. Soon I saw them both walking into the hospital. I waited in the van for about 45 minutes, and my father finally came out of the hospital. He had a smile on his face, but all the way to the van he was shaking his head sideways (like he was saying, "No, I can't believe it"). He got in the van with me and said, "I just paid that man's debt, and it was exactly $1,000!" The thing you don't know is that our family hadn't had any food for almost two weeks because we didn't have any money. Then my father gently said, "Magie, this is living by faith, and I trust and give everything to God, because I know that he always provides."*

When we got back home, people from a nearby town called Ario had brought us food to help us survive for the week. We didn't go without, because my father believed that day.

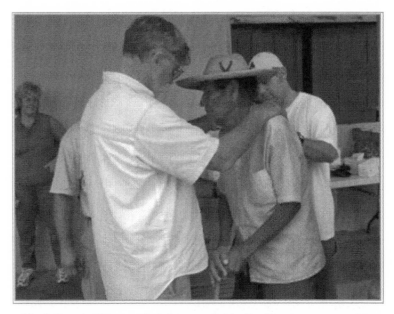

My father uplifting and giving medical attention to a peasant in rural Mexico

Growing up in the orphanage, we always had to be very watchful about scorpions. They were everywhere, especially when it got cold outside, as they would come in the house looking for warmth. Before we would go to sleep, we always checked our beds, and we would also check our shoes every time we put them on. I had the habit of sticking my hand very quickly inside my shoe and pulling it out, to make sure they were no scorpions in it. Through my life there, I got stung eleven different times, and every single time was very painful. After the very first time I got stung, I learned how to deal with a scorpion sting and how to treat myself, and I showed my brothers and sisters how to treat themselves too. If I got stung in my hand, for example, I would completely relax to prevent the poison from spreading quickly, then I would tie my shoelace right above the sting and stick my hand in very cold water to slow the process of the poison spreading.

When the poison spread up my arm, I could actually feel it moving up through the pain, and I would move the shoelace up a little more, until the pain stopped.

One night, one of my newly adoptive brothers got stung by a scorpion in his butt. My parents were out of town and there was no one to treat him, and I thought to myself, "What can I possibly do?" I couldn't tie a shoelace on his butt, so I did the only thing that could save his life. Driven by the fact that I had seen most of my father's patients almost die of scorpion stings, I took him to the down to the river that night, which was about ¼ of a mile down from where the dorms were. I took his clothes off and took him in my arms into the cold river. My idea was to stick most of his body permanently in the cold water to try to slow the poison from spreading. I had seen some of my father's patients almost die of a scorpion sting, and I was not going to let this happen to my newly adoptive brother. He began to shake tremendously, and I wasn't sure if the poison was having an effect on him, or if it was just the cold water. I was at peace as long as he didn't start foaming from his mouth. I will always remember that night... I kept telling him over and over again, "Believe that you are going to be ok!" and he continuously replied, "Yes!" as he steadily kept looking into my eyes. I had complete Faith in what I was doing, and I knew if I could keep his mind believing that he would be ok, and so he was.

A NEW BEGINNING

When I first arrived in the United States, I didn't know any English. I went almost directly into college to study the profession of Interior Design. It was very challenging for me to learn this new language. It was like learning how to read and write again. Even though my parents are originally from the US, the reason they never taught us English in Mexico was because they only spoke it when they would argue, so that we wouldn't understand. It was a blessing to be at the University of Charleston. There was no one there that spoke Spanish, so I learned English very well. I learned English through watching TV and meeting with my teachers after every class for one hour so I could understand them. I remember that my mouth would get sore and sometimes swell up from trying to use new muscles when learning and speaking English. That is because in Spanish we use the front of our mouths, and in English you use the back of your mouths when speaking. My mother later found out how difficult it was for me and my sister to learn English when we came here, so she started speaking English to all of my siblings in Mexico. I am truly amazed by how fluent some of them are now, even the younger kids at the orphanage.

At the University of Charleston, I played basketball on a scholarship, and later received a scholarship to play soccer and to row crew. In basketball, we were conference champions one year, I received the honorable mention of the conference award for soccer and won four medals in rowing crew.

The University of Charleston's Women's Soccer Team. From left to right, I am the second person in the front row wearing the #2 jersey

I was the running midfielder for the Soccer Team

I rowed a single boat, a four-person boat, and an eight-person boat with all guys, winning four medals in different competitions

After our team won several medals at the Governor's Cup. From left to right, I am the last person to the right.

Playing sports in college was an adventure. I had never played real organized basketball or soccer before, and certainly never rowed crew. There, I learned the importance of discipline and accountability that helped propel me in the successful business world. In college, I was part of several organizations, and I received many other awards, honors, scholarships, and was involved in helping the community; I also worked part time cutting grass and trees. I wanted to help my father pay for my education as much as I could.

A few years later, I graduated with a degree in Interior Design and started working for an Interior Design company in Charleston. I started making my fresh salsas and dips, and all of my friends always told me, "You should sell this stuff!" I always told them, "You are nuts!" because it cost me at the time about $40 to make one gallon of salsa with ingredients bought at a local grocery store, and about 3 hours to hand chop it and prepare it completely. We now cut one five-gallon bucket in 20 seconds!

BEING HOMELESS

Before starting my business, I became homeless. I lived out of my station wagon for a few months one winter. I used to lower the seats in the back to make a flat surface so I could make a bed to sleep in. I remember how it got so cold at night that I would turn the car and the heat on high. When the car got really warm, I would then turn it off. During the night, the cold would wake me up, and I would l turn my car on again to stay warm.

Weeks later, I was driving up a hill and my car engine blew up. Flames and smoke were coming out of the engine, so I quickly grabbed my bags and got out. That was the beginning of my life on the street and into the woods for the next several months.

One morning several years later, I was delivering my products to a local supermarket and a woman in line at the checkout counter yelled my name. As she approached me, she said to me, "Magie, I remember when you used to be homeless, and look at where you are now!" In complete humbleness and with deep emotion, I held her hand and dropped to one knee, realizing the blessing of where I used to be, and I said to her, "Thank you".

I didn't realize I was homeless because that's how I lived most of my life at the orphanage. After talking to her for a while, I realized she was the person who caught me sleeping on the street, and I remembered who she was. She was one of the cooks who worked for the University of Charleston that happened to pass by me one day. In 2015, the University of Charleston inducted me into the Hall of Fame, and she was present with me to celebrate (as shown in the picture below).

THE AHA MOMENT

In 2004, my friends pushed me to enter a salsa competition in the state of West Virginia, and I won the contest by unanimous vote.

Market Chat

News from CAPITOL MARKET August 2004

Summer Salsa Contest Results

Thank you to all the contestants for participating in this year's Summer Salsa Contest! The Summer Salsa Contest was a great success and we all had a great day of tasting great salsas, listening to Combo Latino play Latin/Salsa tunes, The Jolly Juggler excited the audience with his performance and the kids enjoyed the face painting.

The winners are:

First Place: Maggie Cook
Second Place: Jerry Workman
Third Place: Bobby Collins
People's Choice Award: Bobby Collins

WV Summer Produce!

This was my AHA moment. I thought to myself, "Maybe I do have something here." At that time, I didn't have any money at all to start this business, and I was deep into debt, but then someone came into my life and gave me $800 to start my business. In that moment, I started to do all the research I needed to start a fresh salsa business, and in July of 2004, Maggie's Salsa LLC was formed. When I did my research, I found that I would be the ONLY fresh salsa company in the state of West Virginia, and one of very few fresh salsa companies in the country. This was my driving factor, this was my uniqueness, this was my niche. When I met with the Department of Agriculture, who works closely with the FDA and its regulations, their marketing person helping with the project kept insisting to me that I should cook my salsa. She said, "Your products will last longer. If you don't cook them, you are going to have trouble selling them with such a short shelf life." At the time, my products only had a shelf life of 15 days. I firmly told her, "No, my products are unique, and I want to keep them fresh-fresh." Now every time I see her, she tells me, "Magie... Remember when I told you that you should cook your salsa, and you said, 'No!' and look at what you have done!" The difference between our products and a jarred product of salsa is that we do not cook our ingredients at all, and they don't come from canned goods, either. Our products are Fresh-Fresh, just as if you were pulling your tomatoes from your garden and chopping them immediately to make salsa. I found that a jarred product of salsa lasted 3-6 years on the shelf, and also found that there were hundreds of jarred salsas on the shelves already.

I am sitting in the FDA approved kitchen that I traveled to every night after work. I drove two hours (back and forth) to get there.

In the beginning of this journey, I had no idea how to start a business or how to run one, but that didn't stop me. When I went to college, I only took one business class,

Business 101, and that was all. I tried contacting other fresh salsa companies to get start up information, but I didn't hear back from them. I was determined to take small baby steps each day to learn everything that was to know about starting a business, and Google became my main source for research. When I started this company, I did everything. I bought the program to design my product labels, I created my own website, and I even got my truck driver's license and drove the product to the stores. The $800 that was given to me was the best-spent $800 I have ever had, and the business didn't get in debt.

Out of the 21 different items we currently have, these are some of the most popular salsa flavors we sell

MAGIE COOK

6

Perseverance

Many of us stall and give up when we want something and we are told, "No, you can't get it," "No, you can't have it," or "No, you can't do it." We give up. We throw in the towel. This is the difference between success and failure. We start to *think*, "They're right, I can't do it," instead of *thinking*, "I have the divine right to obtain all of my heart's desires, and I will keep trying until I achieve success." Faith is the result of something beautiful! Especially when no one believes in you and you still come through with great success. Overcoming adversity is one of my life's greatest accomplishments.

"NO" IS NEVER FOREVER

After I started my food manufacturing business in 2004, my products were ready to go, and all I had to do was to contact as many supermarkets as I could find and sell my products to them. I started by making a very long list of stores that I would call from what I considered the smallest supermarkets to the largest ones. I began an extensive period of cold calling. I felt defeated when the first 90 stores told me "NO, we don't want your products." No one had ever heard of my company, and they were not interested in the "fresh" concept of my products. I stopped calling at my 90 rejections from supermarkets. I picked up the phone and called several food manufacturers to ask them what they had done to get their products in supermarkets. They all told me, "They are not going to listen to you," and one of them said, "It took us 5 years to get in one supermarket." My best friend then, who is a very smart business person, and my business partner now told me, "Why are you doing this; why are you working so hard? You are not making any money. You should just stop doing it."

I was faced with a lot of resistance and disappointment at that time. The only thing I had going for me was the fact that I had very good products, but I wasn't getting anywhere with them.

I remained very strong. I didn't let everyone's

rejections or opinions bring me down. Instead, I kept trying. Yes, it didn't feel very good when I heard, "No, we are not interested in your products," and my confidence was starting to fail. But I kept trying, because I believed in myself when no one believed in me; I believed in my products when no one believed in my products, and all I needed was a breakthrough. I had the realization that a rejection was just a rejection. A simple "No" didn't feel so good, but it didn't mean that I was taking a step backwards; I was still in the same place, so I kept trying.

At that point, I took the list of stores I had created, and turned it upside down, so now what I considered to be the largest supermarket in the US was at the very top of my list. This Supermarket was The Whole Foods Market, the largest organic supermarket chain in the US. I made a cold call, and left a message that said, "Hi, my name is Magie; I have an awesome Pico De Gallo Salsa product that I think you would love. Please contact me if you are interested in trying our products." The next day, I got a call back from them saying, "Magie, we read about you; we want to try your products, when can you come?" I said, "When do you meet next?" They said, "Tomorrow at 9:00 am." I said, "I'll be there!" It was 6:00 pm the night before when they called me, so I literally packed up my car with salsa and drove all night long to Maryland, where I met with the buyers the next day. When I presented my products to them, the room was filled with excitement and the taste testing went exceptionally well! They immediately asked me, "When can we have your products in our stores?" I responded with chills all over my body, "As soon as I can!" At that time, I was making about 200 pounds of salsa per week, selling it to my friends in the area, and I was traveling every night after work to an FDA kitchen that was an hour away to make our products. The Whole Foods Market's first order was for 10,000 pounds of product! I thought to myself, "I have to cut roughly 60,000 tomatoes!"

A Whole Foods shelf display where all of our products were placed on the top shelf

At that time, I had become Vice President of Ridgeview Design, an Interior Design company in the area and was teaching Computer Aided Drafting and Design at the University of Charleston.

The next day, I went to work and resigned my Interior Design position, to take on Maggie's Salsa LLC full time, and the rest was history!

It was a miracle! I had persevered! When it seemed like there was no hope, and all of the odds were against me, I held on to the belief in myself and the biggest breakthrough of my life happened! To make 10,000 pounds of salsa in one week was very exciting! I only had one other helper, and we worked diligently every day to make all the salsa. By the end of the week we both were sore, and our hands felt stiff from filling so many containers by hand.

The belief in my own mind about achieving success was set. It didn't matter how many rejections I got, or how many people told me I couldn't do it. Because of our tremendous growth and business success after this first breakthrough, in 2009 Maggie's Salsa LLC was awarded the Small Business Administration Young Entrepreneur of the Year Award.

In 2009, Maggie's Salsa was awarded the Small Business
Administration Young Entrepreneur of the Year Award. In this
photo, I am standing with my business partner, Rebecca
Warnick. She has been a tremendous asset to Maggie's
Salsa, helping us grow without getting in debt for the first six
years.

A PIECE OF WOOD BLOCK

The next step for me was to find a refrigerated truck to put all of my product in and to drive it to Maryland. I searched all week and finally found a truck. This was the very first truck I had ever rented. The truck was very old and had a lot of rust. I remember there were wires coming out of the dashboard, and the seat was so rusted it was impossible to adjust it. The truck was a manual transmission, and the shifter was so old and wobbly I couldn't tell where the gears were.

The truck was finally loaded and ready to go. I got in it, and with excitement I started to drive down the road. Then I realized that being 5'2" I could barely touch the gas pedal and I was getting ready to go up a very steep hill. When I tried to go up the hill, the truck started to jerk back and forth because I couldn't reach the pedal. I looked around the street and people were laughing at me. I could barely get the truck going, a tremendous agony came over me, and I started to sweat very quickly. I finally got the truck up the hill, and I made the decision to pull over. I said to myself, "I have to figure out how I am going to drive this truck to Maryland." I walked around to the side of the road and I found a piece of wood block. I remembered that I had duct tape in the truck because I had taped one of the mirrors that was about to fall off. So, I took that piece of wood block and duct taped it to my foot and drove 8 hours that night to Maryland to make the delivery on time. On our second delivery, we had to rent the same truck; this time it had a hole in the oil tank, and we had to stop every so often to keep re-filling it, and we later found that it also had a hole in the diesel tank. I had persevered so much during this time that these truck incidents were not even a challenge, they were an adventure!

Obtaining a contract with The Whole Foods Market, (largest organic retailer in the US) opened the door for distribution at the national level with other supermarkets. Because we were doing business with The Whole Foods Markets, other supermarkets wanted to do business with us. This was a great start of an ongoing journey!

7
Inspired Action

You already know that you have the amazing power to manifest your desires by virtue of what you think, feel, and see yourself as, but when you practice *Inspired Action*, you unleash the power of DIVINE interaction. Everything that you want in your life starts falling into place, like pieces coming together in a puzzle.

Inspired Action is to *"act as if"*. When you take Inspired Action, you physically *create* and *live* the experiences you want to manifest, *"acting as if"*. You go to the dealership and ask to drive that car you want to manifest, without limiting yourself in thinking about how much it costs, you buy a one-million-dollar bill online and put it in your wallet, or write yourself a check, and feel like you have achieved your million dollars. You dress like, carry yourself like, and speak like the professional in the position you want to manifest.

If you want something in your life you've never had, you'll have to do something you've never done. –JD Houston

---

BECOME IT TO MANIFEST IT

When I graduated college, I graduated with an Interior Design degree from the University of Charleston. I did some research about the Interior Design Market in the state of West Virginia and found that 95% of Interior Design graduates in this state either moved out of state to take a job or couldn't find a job at all. I was very surprised by this fact, but I still went and pursued getting a job with a local company. I got the job, but the pay was very minimum for me, and I was struggling to make ends meet, living paycheck to paycheck. Then a deep desire for change sparked in me. I said to myself, "It is time for a change!" I wanted to change physically and mentally. Rooted by the deep desire to change, I sat down, grabbed a piece of paper and wrote two very powerful affirmations. They read:

"I am joyfully experiencing a fulfilled life as President or Vice President of an Interior Design firm or something better."

"I am gratefully living to my fullest potential and creating the change that I want to be."

From that moment on, I decided to begin a journey of total transformation. I wanted to become a well-paid and successful professional Interior Designer. I made a choice to carry myself like a professional Interior Designer, and to dress like one. I didn't have a lot of money, but I took everything I had and went shopping at a local consignment store. I bought the best professional clothes I could find, even if some of them had holes on them.

At work, my co-workers started to notice that something was different about me. Some of them asked me, "What is going on with you?" I looked beautiful dressed in designer clothes and in high heels bought in a consignment shop. I got a gym membership and started eating the healthiest foods I could find. Every morning right when I arrived to work, I sat down at my computer and became so moved with desire when I read my affirmations. I was so emotional about achieving this that I would passionately shed some tears in the process of visualizing it every single day. About 29 days later, I got invited to lunch with a group of business people. In that group, I met a man who had a construction business and who was starting up an Interior Design business to complement his construction business. Right then and there, he asked me if I would become Vice President of his Interior Design! I got chills all over my body! I couldn't believe it!! I said, "YES!" I went on to help design and build multimillion-dollar homes at the Greenbrier Resort in West Virginia, along with several commercial and government projects in the area.

Here I am standing in a company advertisement as Vice President of Ridgeview Design

I used *Inspired Action* to manifest my desires. *I made my **future** dream a **present fact**, by **assuming** the **feeling** of my **wish fulfilled!** I **enveloped** myself in my **desire** and my **joy was full.** I **made peace with it** within my Spirit, and I manifested it into my life, in only 29 days!* This was Inspired Action in action.

The power of attraction in *Inspired Action* is one of the most effective ways for manifesting your desires. It can be far more effective than any other method for manifestation because you are physically putting yourself in the position you want to eventually manifest, and when you do, you begin to *believe* that you are *already there*; you are invocating one of the most powerful laws in the Universe, *The Law of Attraction.* You are *affirming* your *faith* in the manifestation of what you want to see.

Inspired Action can be far more effective than visualization, because you are physically there. Your feel-good emotions are at an all-time high, and your mind is saying, "I can feel it, see it, touch it, and smell it, it is here, it is done."

You can practice *Inspired Action* along with vision boards, affirmations, visualization, and meditation. In the following chapters, we will discuss the power of vision boards, affirmations, visualization, and meditation. Your ultimate goal is to test and try every single method for success and decide what works best for you. What works for you may not work for everyone, so explore and enjoy!

MAGIE COOK

8
Mindful Goals

What is it that you wish to accomplish in your lifetime that will give you true exhilarating joy, a sense of peace, and happiness? For some, success might mean the accomplishment of feeling constant joy through the mastery of meditation, being in perfect health, buying a piece of land on the ocean, living a peaceful life with your partner and pets, graduating from college, owning a home, starting a business, owning a business that makes you money effortlessly and automatically, becoming a millionaire, getting married, starting a family, or perhaps it is finding your life's purpose and living it.

Success is taking the first step and writing down your goals, even if you can't see the end result. Writing down your goals is the beginning process for unleashing your true power. It is the birth of all of your accomplishments. It is the one thing that connects you to everything you want to become. Taking this first step is very important, but it is also very important to remember *who you really are*, to *believe* in yourself, and lastly, in order to truly live the life that you desire, you must discover what your *life's purpose* is, and begin to live it!

TAKE THE FIRST STEP

I was driving one afternoon on the interstate on my way to Charleston when a big storm hit. The storm was so strong that all I could see was approximately two feet in front of me. My goal was to get to Charleston, and the only things guiding me were the barely visible white lines on the road. I became filled with emotion because I was living in the moment. That experience was teaching me something very important. I understood that even though I could only see two feet in front of me, I was going to make it home. I didn't have to see the whole road, all I had to do was follow the white lines on the road and trust that I would get there.

We often get discouraged because we cannot see the destination. You must have a clear, defined vision of your goals, a belief in attaining them, and a road map to follow and stay on until you get there, even if you can't physically see the end result. How fast you get there depends on how well you *plan, visualize, expect,* and *believe* in your end result.

You must *believe* in yourself, *remember who you really are,* and be confident that if you take the steps each day towards your goals for success and happiness, you will arrive at the destination you envision.

BELIEVING IN YOU!

When you can believe in yourself more than your loved ones, more than friends, more than anyone else can, you truly give yourself the gift of all power! One of the most impacting moments for me was when my father told me that I would never amount to anything. That I would die in prison and with AIDS. He was angry about something serious, just like any parent would be, and he probably didn't mean what he said at that time, but when I heard those words, I hurt deep inside. I made a decision that moment to stand firm, and I tightened my fists and said to myself, "I will be a success, and I will show him!", and indeed I did! I never forgot his words, and I tried so hard not to let them influence my reality.

Because of this incident, I developed the fear of failure. So, every time someone would tell me that I couldn't do something, I did it with complete success. My friends know this.

I went hiking with a family once in the Rocky Mountains of West Virginia. Along the way, we found an awesome deep and wide hole in the ground. It was a cave, but it was down in the ground. I decided to explore it and fell in it. When I tried to get out, the family that I was with could not reach my hands, and there was nothing around to pull me out with. I panicked because I also had a fear of spaces I couldn't get out of. I had this fear because I got stuck in a deep cave in Mexico for a half a day. It was the most horrifying of experiences. My father in Mexico would ask me and my brothers to pull the puppy dogs out of the caves from the steep mountainside hills at the ranch where the orphanage was. That is where the dogs had their puppies to keep them hidden and protected. So now I was stuck in a cave in the Mountains of West Virginia, when one of the guys in our group said four words that triggered my entire being: "She can't do it!" He said it because he knew what triggered me. I jumped out of that cave like a monkey in a split second. I was shocked at myself, and so were they. His wife smacked him in the arm and said, "I can't believe you did that." Those words worked like magic.

What my father said to me that day was perfect! I chose to use his words to build me, not destroy me. It taught me a few lessons in life. One of the lessons was to stay strong and accomplish anything I set my mind to, to believe in myself. It made me the person that I am today. Because all of my life I struggled with trying to impress him in any way I could, I always worked extra hard to do it, and when he passed, I thought to myself, "Who am I going to impress now?" At that moment I realized that I didn't need to impress anyone, that the person I needed to make happy was me. I also understood very clearly my partnership and connection to God, and how I could not break away from that unity. I broke away from having the fear of failure, and when I did this, I really started enjoying life to the fullest. I made a promise to always stay true to myself, and to always believe in myself.

LIVING YOUR PURPOSE

When I was in middle school, I developed a tremendous interest in the game of basketball. I loved it so much that I started practicing on my own. It became my passion, my purpose. My desire to become the best basketball player in my school was born. I was never coached or trained on how to play basketball; I simply watched other people play and tried to watch as many games as I could, to learn how to dribble, shoot the ball and perform all of my moves. The coach I had in middle school was the physical education teacher. He simply let us play with the ball and do anything we wanted. I would practice at home for at least four hours or more per day. Before we had a concrete basketball court, we had a dirt court with a wire hoop for a basket nailed to a post. Basketball became such a passion to me that I would invent drill scenarios in my mind to become the best basketball player I couldbe.

I was practicing on the court one afternoon, and one of my adoptive brothers was sitting on the sidelines watching me play. He had a condition called spinal bifida and couldn't walk, so he just sat there for a few hours watching me play. Then I thought of something. I said, "Pancho, I am going to cover my eyes completely with this piece of rag; every time I get to the edge of the court, can you tell me to stop and turn"? He said, "Sure, Magie." So, I started dribbling the ball at full speed, doing crossovers, going behind my back, doing half-turn body rotations with the ball, and Pancho was doing really well at stopping me when I got near the edge, but Pancho stopped helping me. I stepped on the ledge and fell down the hill and off the court. I asked Pancho, "Why didn't you tell me I was near the edge?" He said, "Because you are dribbling so well that I thought you were watching." I said, "No, I am totally blind; please help me again, okay?" So, I began dribbling the ball again at full speed, and after a while, Pancho stopped helping me again. This time, I hit the wood post with my head and had to get three stitches in my forehead. I was so passionate about the game of basketball that I was very inventive, and would try almost anything, I would daydream, and even sleep with my ball at night. I would do anything to achieve my dream of becoming the best basketball player in my school. We went on to win all the games and championships in my years in middle school, and later, many games and championships in high school. In high school, I would play one-on-one basketball in any break time we had with all the guys in my school for tacos and tortas. Yes! Tacos and Mexican sandwiches! It was awesome. I had some moves that were amazing; when the ball would go in, they thought they were lucky shots, but they weren't. My passion had become a success, because I made every opportunity count for me. I was living on purpose. Because my basketball talents grew, I later got recruited to play basketball for the Mexican National Team in Mexico City, but couldn't go because I broke my collarbone. However, my dream to play college basketball with a scholarship still came through because I believed in myself.

Discovering your purpose is the driving force of all of your dreams, goals, and all of your future accomplishments! Having purpose will allow you to create momentum and build your motivation; it will give you *Inspired Action*, it will sharpen your intuition, and it will move you to *act by faith* in all of your endeavors. If at first it seems like there is not a way, you find a way, and make things happen. You are so inspired by your purpose that you think about ways to achieve success in every way that you can possibly think of. You are submerged in your new reality. You think about your goals all of the time and you become in tune with your higher self. Ideas and solutions to your problems begin manifesting while you are dreaming at night, and you have a pen and paper ready to jot down the solutions the next morning. It becomes very exciting when everything that moves you starts each day from your fire within. Everything seems surreal, you feel like you are in another world (your own creation), you feel elated, exhilarated, you keep writing and rewriting your daily goals and putting your accomplishments in a victory log. You track your progress and reward yourself for it. If someone tells you that you can't do something, you say, "I can, and I'll show you." You feel unstoppable.

This is what it feels like to live on Purpose, this is what it feels like to live in Spirit.

Everyone was born with a life purpose. If you ask any 4-year-old what they want to be when they grow up, they almost jump out of their seat to tell you with excitement what they want to become someday. Everyone was born with that seed, that feeling within to strive to create themselves in life, but something happened along the way. It got turned off. You forgot *who you really are*, and you live life on autopilot, based on the early programming instilled by your loved ones or our experiences along the way.

When you are on purpose, you are in constant attracting mode. You are magically attracting the people, the circumstances, and ideas into your life. It almost seems like it happens so effortlessly. You are turned on. Since most of the thoughts you are thinking are aligned with your purpose, so are your deep passionate feelings and vision, and you begin to manifest almost instantly. The people that are around you can tell that you look different, because you are shining; they see light, inspiration, they see enthusiasm, and they are stimulated by you. They love you for it, they want to help you, and they want to be around you more.

My life's purpose is to *use love and compassion to create products and services that inspire and transform people's minds to end suffering.* My goal is to help prepare the fertile soil to plant a seed in people's minds through this book, and the future series of Mindful Success™ Books, through my seminars, my inspiring keynote speeches, and inspirational products and services that you can find on our website.

Ever since I was a little kid, I had a tremendous compassion to give and to help others, so much that it became a problem for me. When my father had a little more money, he would buy my brothers and I little things like hunting knives, and sometimes little cars to play with. Sometimes he would give me things from his childhood, like bows and arrows he made on his own, and other fun memories. When we would get a visitor at our home and they wanted my knives or toys, I would simply give them away, because they showed so much interest that I felt they would appreciate and love them better than me. It felt good to do it, too. When my father would find out, he would take the knives or toys back from them and would try to give me a lesson about keeping my things. He did this because I literally gave away everything I had. I had watched him do it with the poor, and I was doing what he was doing. He got upset because he considered what he gave me to be very valuable to him.

Two years after I arrived in the US, I was walking at night in the streets of Charleston. I had just bought a pair of the newest Air Jordans and I was very happy because I had worked so hard to get them. It was raining that evening, and I was walking with an umbrella. On a street corner, I saw a homeless woman lying on the street trying to cover herself from the rain. I also noticed that she didn't have any shoes. I approached her and asked her if I could give her my shoes and my umbrella, and she said yes. I took my shoes and socks off and helped her put them on her feet. To my surprise, my shoes fit her perfectly, and I had the biggest smile on my face. I also began to shed some tears, because I was experiencing a tremendous amount of compassion for her and I wished I could have done more. I proceeded to walk about one mile to get to the place where I was staying, and during that time period I kept shedding tears and felt like I was sharing in that woman's suffering. It was the most amazing experience for me! When I walked up to the door of the home where I was staying, my friend opened the door and saw that I was completely soaked and with no shoes. She went crazy about what I had done. She couldn't believe it, because she knew how much I loved those shoes. In that moment, she reminded me of my father, but I knew that what I had done really helped someone else, and I was at peace.

Once my manufacturing business became a success, we became supporters of my parents' orphanage and organization for the poor in Mexico. One summer day in 2011, I began getting calls and messages from several of my adoptive brothers and sisters in the orphanage. They said, "Magie, we have only had sugar and lettuce to eat for two weeks. We are hungry, can you help us?" I lost it! I started to shed some very strong compassionate tears. This immediately took me back to the times when I was growing up and how I was hungry for long periods of time. Because of this incident, we created a movement called Pound 4 Pound (for every pound of food we sell of selective products, one pound of food is donated to hungry children around the world). With this movement, we have been able to buy dried goods like beans, rice, powdered milk, and many other products to feed hungry kids in Mexico.

In his book, "The Success Principles", Jack Canfield asks his readers to answer one very important question: *"What is a job I would love so much that I'd do*

it for free, but I could actually get paid for it?" Take a moment to review and meditate upon this. Can you answer this very simple question? If you can, you may have just found your life's purpose!

This was very interesting, but very powerful. Most of our lives, we live by settling for less than what we want, or we go the route that our parents and family members want for us, but some of us win because we choose to make the best of every opportunity, and when we do this, life takes us on the most wonderful unexpected journey.

In his younger years, my father wanted to be a boxer. He started fighting in the ring and became a golden glove boxer, with an opportunity to go to the Olympics. His father told him that he was not going to support him with his dream, that his life would not amount to anything, he said that his life would have no future in boxing, that he had a better life becoming a medical doctor. Even though my father had a successful beginning in boxing, he listened to his father and went to medical school, and eventually became a research scientist for NASA. In my father's case, he still became a great success in life. I am very much like him. He chose to become something greater than he first imagined; he went on to help and heal millions of poor people in the rural towns of Mexico for 38 years and changed the lives of millions of people through preaching the message of God.

My father (on the right) when he was a golden glove boxer. He always described this fight as intimidating because his opponent was in a heavier weight class than he was. That day, he knocked his opponent out with one single punch.

The point I am trying to make here is that most people get STUCK in their lives by doing something they don't want to do. They may have gotten there on their own or they were conditioned to be where they are by their parents' early childhood conditioning. But every one of us has a choice; a choice to be free and feel complete inner happiness!

If you are longing to discover your life's purpose and have a deep passion within to change your current circumstances and become a success, you must listen to your inner self. You must remember *who you really are.* You must understand that you become limitless when you get in touch with your higher self, which is the connection to "All that Is", which is the connection to God.

You can begin to ask yourself these questions:

"What is it that I really want in life?"

"What makes me exhilarated and happy?"

"What are my unique personal qualities that I can turn into my life's purpose?"

"What are the ways I enjoy expressing those qualities when interacting with others?"

You can start by writing a list of things that move you deeply and passionately.

Ask and it will be given to you; seek and you will find; knock and the door will be opened to you. Matthew 7:7

A very powerful choice to make is to apply meditation in the search of your life's purpose. Go within and ask God for guidance and revelation. When you know how to ask, God always answers! You can enter into meditation, quiet your mind, and open yourself completely to God; you must enter into a deep state of self-love and peace, and in silence, ask:

"What is my purpose for living?"

"Why am I here?"

"What is my role in this Universe?"

Have a pen and paper available. Be patient; be at peace, your answers will come when you are ready *(For more information on purpose meditations visit MagieCook.com).*

WRITING SUCCESSFUL GOALS

When writing your goals, the most powerful thing you are doing is unleashing the creative magic power that is born within your entire being. To my experience, I believe that the best way to write your goals is with a pen and paper. I have always felt a very strong connection between my hand and my brain. It feels as if my goals are being imprinted in my mind as I begin writing them. When I hand write my goals, it takes me a little longer, therefore I contemplate them a little longer. I have also found that most people, when they use a pen and paper, tend to quietly speak as they write. Writing my goals has given me tremendous success in life.

Once you have determined what your life purpose is, and you have a vision of what you want to achieve, you have to take your desires and convert them into specific, measurable goals, and as soon as you write them, you can start acting on them for their completion. It is important to acknowledge that when you write your goals, you are unleashing your power for success. You are giving to your Subconscious mind a task, and it will work 24 hours per day, 7 days per week to achieve what you desire. Remember that the more you re-read and re-visit your goals, the more heighten their impact on your subconscious mind. The highest impact that your goals will have on your subconscious mind occurs right before you go to bed or right after you awaken.

When your brain is getting ready for sleep, it reaches the Alpha level of mind, making the principle of autosuggestion an effective way to deeply root your desires into your subconscious mind. The most effective method for achieving your results is meditation. When you enter into meditation, you also reach the Alpha level of mind. I encourage you to record your goals and play them with smooth background music. You may want to purchase the Alpha sound to include it in the background. Listening to the Alpha sound will help you get into the Alpha level of the mind much quicker. You can purchase Alpha sounds from SilvaMethod.com.

The great impact for success here is that you are actually listening to your goals while you are at the Alpha level of mind, while your Subconscious mind is at the highest levels of receptivity.

Here are the steps to take in writing successful goals.

1. You must make them as specific as possible. If you want a new home, what is the type of home you want, what are the colors, materials, features that you want in it? Successful goals are specific goals.

2. You must make your goals measurable and clear. You must add a specific time and date to it. For example, "I will weigh 125 pounds by 1 pm on May 25." When you are not setting criteria for measurement, it becomes only a wish; this is the only way to truly engage your Subconscious mind.

Here are more examples of good written goals:

- I will be on the Dr. Oz show sharing my story and success by 3:00 pm, January 2015

- I will make $1,000,000 dollars gross profit by 5:00 pm, March 15, 2015

- I will purchase a 5,000 square foot home on the island of Jamaica by noon, April 30, 2017

DAILY SUCCESS GOALS

When I started my food manufacturing business, I was working full-time for an Interior Design firm, and I was also teaching Computer Aided Drafting and Design at the University of Charleston. Every night after teaching *the class, I would drive for 45 minutes to a different town where they had an FDA-certified kitchen where I could make my products. I would come back home sometimes at one or two in the morning and be up by 5 am again to tackle the day. During any down time, I had, I would write and re-write my daily goals to stay focused. I did this for over a year. The system that I will be revealing to you in the following pages helped me stay organized and prioritized in my personal and business life. It has been the most effective way to generate the quickest results for me, helping me accomplish so much in such a short period of time. This system was very instrumental in helping me start my manufacturing business with $800 and grow it without going in debt.*

It is very important that you write daily goals, that is, what you want to accomplish on a day-to-day basis. Writing your goals will heighten your intuition and speed the process of the direction you want to go. It is the beginning of all of your instant manifestations.

This is my favorite and most exciting daily process, because I get to accomplish so many things. I get to write the word "Victory" next to my accomplished goals, or I get to mark them off of my list. I have used a daily goal spreadsheet system for years. It has helped me achieve in one year what most people achieve in 3 to 5 years. This system is based on the 80/20 rule, the **law of the vital few,** in which 20 percent of the goals are always responsible for 80 percent of the results.

When I saw the success I had with it, I introduced it to my office team. At first, they were very resistant, but later they were amazed at how much they got done in one day. They became believers in daily goal achievement through this system. This daily goal spreadsheet system helps you stay on track each day, it helps you stay organized, and it helps you take care of the most important things that have the most value in accomplishing first. I write and re-write my goals sometimes 3-5 times daily, because situations may occur during the course of the day where I may need to change my game plan and re-evaluate what the most important things are. This type of daily goal setting and achievement is very effective.

Here is an example:

Maggie's Daily Goal Spreadsheet

	Date:
MIP (Most Important) Calls	**Follow ups**
1	
2	
3	
Most Important/ Most Urgent	**Follow ups**
1	
2	
3	
Least Important/ Least Urgent	
1	
2	
3	

The best time to write your daily goals is the night before. When you do this, you will be planning your entire day the night before. You will also be activating them with the power of the Subconscious mind if you do this right before you go to sleep.

This system becomes so effective because you have all of your daily goals written on one page, and whether you get them all done in one day or not, they are still there. You get to look at them daily until you get them done. They are there as constant reminders.

Your daily goals do not have to have a completion date, because your goal is to get them started or done that day; however, they do need to be very specific. Sometimes my daily goals will be described as *one simple word.*

I do my daily goal system on an Excel spreadsheet, because if things change during the course of the day, I can simply cut and paste goals to move them where they need to be moved.

The Most Important Calls (MIP calls), Most Important/Most Urgent, and Least Important/Least Urgent goals are always listed from top to bottom, at the top being the ones I believe are the most important ones, and towards the bottom what I consider to be the least important ones. Sometimes things that are in the Least Important/Least Urgent bracket have to be moved to the Most Important/Most Urgent bracket, and so on. On your spreadsheet, you must write your "Follow Ups". Follow ups are very important in completing your goals. Just because you made a call or started working on a High Importance Goal does not mean that your goal is always complete. Sometimes you have to wait for people to call you back to complete your goal or follow up on a goal that involved someone else on the process of its completion.

I also use this system to keep track of what my office team is doing, keeping my business partner accountable, and managing my production team for success. Aside from using this system for business purposes, I also use it for my personal life. Being well-organized in this way about your daily accomplishments is a complete relief; it takes the worry out of your day. You know what you are supposed to do next because you simply see the next thing on the list, and it also takes away the worry of forgetting to do something important.

One of the reasons my office team was hesitant at first about this system was because when they started, it took them about 30 minutes to gather their thoughts and put everything in order each morning, but once they realized that they had the entire day organized, all they had to do was move from one goal to the next without thinking about it, without having stacks of paper all over their desk, trying to figure out what to do next. It was a relief for them, and they were getting so much done with no difficulty whatsoever. A perfectly well-organized day is a free-flowing day. It will relieve you of a lot of stress and allow you to enjoy your progress so much more.

My goal each day is to get as many Most Important/Most Urgent goals accomplished as possible, and my favorite part is being able to cross them off or write the word "Victory" right beside them if they are my biggest goals.

One very important tool for success I have used for the past few years is a voice recorder, which is part of my smartphone. When I am going about my day, I always encounter situations that turn into a daily goal, and I simply record it as I go along. The following day, I listen to all of my voice memos and I include them in my daily goals sheet. There, I can decide if I need to accomplish it myself or if it needs to be delegated.

Just as it is very important to keep an uncluttered mind, using meditation for your best daily successful results, it is important to keep an uncluttered desk. Having an uncluttered desk will keep you peaceful in your daily operations, and your energy will flow much better through your office. You will feel clear, accomplished, and happier if you keep a well-organized and clean office space.

100 LIFETIME GOALS

I started writing my goals when I was living in the orphanage in Mexico. The very first time I wrote my goals, I was in my last year of middle school. Because of my success with my grades, architecture school, and my outstanding performance in basketball, my father had given me a little piece of heaven. He gave me a small office space where I could study and work on any architecture plans. I went on to design a few of his churches in Mexico, including his biggest church in the town of Ario called Maranatha Fellowship, and his Bible institute where he trained his pastors. In this office space, I used the north window to contemplate the sky and write everything that I wanted to become when I grew up. I was meditating and writing goals, and I didn't even know or understand the power behind them!

Before you begin writing your goals, be sure to contemplate what you want in the different areas of your life (financial, business/career, relationships, family/free time, health/appearance, and community). Before you do this, sit down, close your eyes, clear your mind and get into a state of joy and happiness. Start writing your goals as soon as they start coming into your awareness. This process should feel very exhilarating. Everything should feel like it's flowing into you and out onto your paper. I encourage you to keep going until nothing else comes up, then take a break, and come back to continue until you finish. Taking a break will help you regroup and think of any other goal possibilities. Once you have written down 100 goals you want to achieve in your lifetime, make it a point to review them at least once per day. If it is easier for you, write them on 3x5 index cards and carry them around with you, or put them by your bedside at night so you can review them as often as you can. Let me remind you that the more often you review them, the more focus you give them; therefore, your attraction power is increased.

There was a study conducted at the Harvard MBA program in 1979. In the book, "What They Don't Teach You in the Harvard Business School," Mark McCormack tells of the study conducted on students in that program that year. A question that students were asked was, **"Have you set clear, written goals for your future and made plans to accomplish them?"** Only three percent of the graduates had written goals; 13 percent had goals, but they were not in writing; and a whopping 84 percent had no specific goals at all.

Ten years later, the members of the class were interviewed again, and these were the findings: **The 13 percent of the class who had goals were earning, on average, twice as much as the 84 percent who had no goals at all,** and the three percent who had clear, written goals were earning, on average, **ten times as much as the other 97 percent put together**

In the bestseller, *"Goals!"*, Brian Tracy teaches you how to identify in the clearest terms the things you want out of life, then how to make the plan to help you achieve those things. Brian Tracy says there are **four reasons why people don't set goals:**

- They don't realize the importance of goals. If the people with whom you spend the most time — family, friends, colleagues, and so forth — are not clear and committed to goals, there is a chance that you will not be, either.

- They don't know how to set goals. Some set goals that are too general. These are, in reality, fantasies common to everyone. Goals, on the other hand, are clear, written, specific, and measurable.

- They fear failure. Failure hurts, but it is often necessary to experience failure in order to achieve the greatest success. Do not unconsciously sabotage yourself by not setting any goals in which you might fail.

- They fear rejection. People are often afraid that if they are unsuccessful at achieving a goal, others will be critical of them. This is remedied by keeping your goals to yourself at the outset; let others see your results and achievements once you've accomplished your goals

(You can refer to Chapter 8 to read about Writing Successful Goals).

MAJOR BREAKTHROUGH GOAL

When I started my manufacturing company in 2004, I wrote a goal that read, **"I will sell my Fresh Salsas and Dips in big supermarket chains, by July 3, 2007,"** *and so it happened just a little before that date! I didn't know how it was going to happen, and I didn't worry, I just had a goal and the inspiration to pursue it. This goal was so great for me, considering I was holding only $800 in my hand.*

The way that I achieved this goal without getting in debt was my attitude towards it and the action I took. That $800 multiplied in a very amazing way. I would hand chop and make salsa by the gallon and sell it to all of my friends by the pint. Every time I made a sale, I would go, "whoo hoo!" and wave all the one-dollar bills in the air. I would then take that money and reinvest it in making more salsa, and that is how the business grew. At one point, I had a stack, six inches high, of almost all one-dollar bills, and I would admire it and say, "I am abundantly wealthy!" And again, I would shout, "whoo hoo!"

Your major breakthrough goal is something so great that by starting on it now, it will propel you to the next level! It is a deep desire you have with immeasurable joy and purpose. It is something that gives you inspired action. Just by thinking about it, it makes you smile. You already see yourself there, and this inspires you to want to get there even more. You are doing this because you want change, because you are tired of being in the same place as you have been for a long time. It is the one thing that will bring you happiness, wealth, abundance, joy, romance, health, love, and family.

Most of us haven't allowed ourselves to write down what we truly want, because we can't see how we are going to manifest it. I am here to tell you the importance of not worrying about the "hows". When you worry about the "hows," you are always resisting the true nature of that very thing you want.

When you know how to ask, or state something that you want, the Law of Attraction will move all the people, events, and circumstances that manifest what you are asking when you focus your attention to what you want. There are no limits, only the limits you set upon your mind.

"Whether you think you can, or you think you can't - you're right." — Henry Ford

---

In writing your major breakthrough goal, it is important that you take the time to reflect upon what it is that you truly want that would make a dramatic change in your life. Ask yourself, "What is one single change in your business, career, relationship, or lifestyle that would transcend you to the next level?" Is it starting a new business, finding romance, having a breakthrough in sales, developing a new product that becomes a hit, losing 50 pounds, or buying a home?

Once you have written your major breakthrough goal, I encourage you to share your goal and vision with friends, family, and as many people as you can think of. The more you share your goals, the more you will be amazed at the attraction power you can generate for its materialization. Never let anything or anyone tell you that you can't achieve something; if they do, move on to the next person.

When you are ready to embark on your journey, you must create action steps to get started. Use the daily goals spreadsheet described in this chapter, reach for your fire within, believe in your purpose, believe in yourself, remember who you really are and how the mind works, act upon Inspired Action, and be ready to persevere. In the following chapters, we will be talking about very important tools and principles that will add momentum to the accomplishment of your major breakthrough.

MAGIE COOK

9
Vision Boards

THE POWER!

The power of attraction in vision boards is astonishing. Perhaps the best way I have implemented inspired action is through my vision boards. When I started my business in 2004, I was faced with the fact that I didn't know anything about starting a business. I had no idea where to begin, but I was inspired to do anything I could to achieve my goals. So, I created my first vision board. One day, I decided to print pictures from the Internet and cut clippings out of magazines for all of the equipment and resources I needed to really grow my business. My vision board sat right in front of me, next to my office desk. It was the first thing I saw every morning when I came in. Vision boards are such a great asset, especially if you have trouble visualizing what you want to attain. These were clear pictures of what I exactly wanted to manifest for my company. When I started my prosperity meditation each morning with eyes closed, I emotionally got enveloped in my prayer and I would slightly open one eye to look up to my vision board, and I would pray and visualize already having each one of the things on my board. I wanted to buy a big truck, I wanted a big packaging machine for my products, I wanted to move into a big manufacturing plant, I wanted fresh produce distribution from Mexico, and I needed money to buy the packaging for my product and all these other things.

One of the very first things that I needed to purchase was the plastic packaging for my containers. This was the first time I had to purchase packaging for my product (the plastic containers that housed the fresh salsa). I contacted several manufacturers to get the best pricing, and I chose the company with the best pricing, but the problem was that I had to buy a truck load of product to make it happen (roughly 100,000 containers). I had just started my business with $800, and I didn't want to get into debt. I thought to myself, "There has got to be a way for me to make this happen." I sat down and looked at my containers on my vision board, closed my eyes, and in meditation I asked God for help. Soon I got a GREAT IDEA, and I acted with inspired action as soon as I could.

The man I was renting an FDA kitchen from, also sold his products in similar containers as I did. So, I approached him and asked him, "What are you paying for your containers right now?" He said $.34, and I said, "What if I can get them for you at $.14, would you buy a truck load and let me buy them off from you at this price?" His face lit up and he said YES! I used my negotiating skills to bring down the price of the manufacturer who wanted to do business with me the *most. And so it happened. Inspired action through the use of my vision board not only benefited me, but it greatly benefited the owner of the kitchen, because he saved $100,000 on his next purchase, and I got my containers on an as-needed basis and without having to go into debt.*

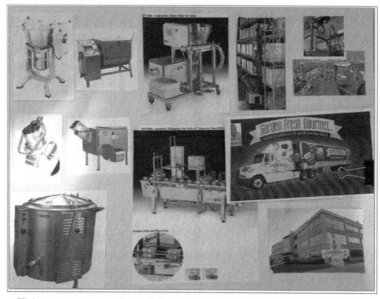

This was my very first vision board. Everything that I placed on this vision board was acquired within a year's time and without getting in debt!

Remember that your Subconscious mind only sees things in pictures! When you plant something in your Subconscious mind, you are setting in motion one of the great laws of the Universe, the Law of Attraction. Your Subconscious is the creator of all the things you want (Spiritual or material). Once something is enveloped by the Subconscious mind, it must manifest, it is law. It

---

must manifest, because that is where your beliefs reside, and when you believe something to be true, that is when the miracle happens. This is a great, powerful technique to achieve your goals!

The power in vision boards lays in the process of visualization. It allowed me to dream; to feel like I was already there, like I was physically holding the things I wanted. The power of Vision boards allows you to visualize with more clarity and power, because you physically see the objects you want to manifest. Every time I looked at my vision board, it felt as if all of these ideas on how to attain my goals started to flow in my head.

I saw the amazing power that vision boards had and the results they brought to my business and decided to try it for my personal life.

My brother Juan had come to visit me one weekend. He came into my office and saw something on my personal vision board that got him very excited. It was a brand-new gray, six speed hard top convertible BMW. When he came back to visit me six months later and walked into my office, he said, "Is that? Haaa! Uhhh!" as he started shrugging his shoulders and rubbing his arms with chills. I said "YES!" My gray, six speed hard top convertible BMW was sitting in the parking lot, completely paid for in full.

By using the power of vision boards, it was easier for me to create a clear mental movie of what I wanted. Not only did I create a clear mental movie of me driving my brand-new car, but I enveloped myself in my own movie. I heard the revving sound of my awesome BMW engine, I felt the exciting vibration of the engine in my body as I pushed on the gas pedal, I felt the amazing grip of my hands on the leather steering wheel, and I was exhilarated when I felt the wind flowing through my hair as I was driving my car with the top down. This was an amazing experience. I felt like I already had the car, like it was a part of me!

Before ultimately manifesting this amazing car into my life, I did something that propelled the magic of attracting it to me even greater. I was exhilarated and full of joy! I used one of the most amazing and powerful techniques called *Inspired Action (refer to Chapter 7 to learn about Inspired Action).*

Inspired action is divine manifestation.

I drove to a luxury car dealership. I walked in with full confidence and headed to the front desk. A salesman was standing there as I pulled a $1,000,000 bill I purchased online from my wallet. I slapped it onto the desk, and I said, "I have one million dollars and I want to test drive that luxurious hard top convertible you have." He rushed to give me the keys immediately, and soon I was test driving my dream car. The experience of using my previous visualizations just got tremendously stronger by the simple act of physically being there having the experience. I took that car and drove it for half of the day with the top down. It was the most exhilarating experience!

I later told my business partner of the experience I had created, and she said to me, "Do you realize that is a car that is over one hundred thousand dollars?" I said, "YES," with a big smile. Being a car salesman for years, she then asked, "Didn't they ask you for proof of your financials?" I said, "NO," again with a big smile. She couldn't believe that they let me drive that car. It was the belief in myself and my confidence that got me into driving that car.

10

Mindful Affirmations

If you are feeling lack about something, understand that this is the birth of a desire. Once this is recognized, you can shift your awareness from feeling "lack" through the use of affirmations to feeling "abundant" within your desire. When you shift your awareness, you become a vibrational match to the essence of your desire. Your vibrational match then irrevocably turns your desire into manifestation.

CREATIVE MAGIC!

The very first time I wrote my affirmations, they changed my life forever. I went from struggling to make ends meet to becoming a vice president of an Interior Design Firm in just 29 days! Since then, I have written my affirmations as creatively as possible. I have found that the more creative I get with them, the more focus and attracting power I am giving to my desires. It becomes a fun process; I allow myself to dream, to see no limitations, and to choose to see the best outcome possible or something better. Affirmations are the creative process of miracles, the magic behind success.

These were some of my affirmations:

"I am joyfully experiencing a fulfilled life as President or Vice President of an Interior Design firm or something better."

"I am gratefully living to my fullest potential and creating the change that I want to be."

I created change not only by writing them, but by living them!

(Refer to Chapter 7 to read about this story).

Affirmations are the strongest tool you can use, and have an amazing attracting power for manifesting your desires. Positive affirmations can be as simple as you want to make them, or they can be very specific and goal-oriented. Affirmations are simple declarations of where you want to be or how you want to feel. They can also help you replace negative, limiting beliefs that you have bought or sold from anyone throughout your life. It takes about 30 days to shift your thought process, to reprogram them, but in order for this to happen, you must read and review them every single day.

Some examples of **positive affirmations** are:

-*I am attracting wealth and abundance into my life.*

-*I am confident, strong, beautiful, powerful, and humble.*

-*I commit to excellence and inner development with love.*

-*I choose to do today, the best I can with what I have.*

-*Every challenge I have is enriching, empowering, and advancing.*

-*The world is plotting to do me good today.*

-*I am attracting all of the people and resources I need for the accomplishment of my goals.*

The secret of all power, all achievement, and all possession lies in the way we think, and in our thoughts exist our deeply rooted *beliefs* that drive our everyday manifestations. If we can remember *who we really are*, we will have the *awareness* and the power to *shift* our thinking and create the life that we want, to let go of the old habits and create new agreements, and you can do this with the use of affirmations.

When we tap into our *higher self*, in which we have access to the GREAT POWER of God, and become aware of the wisdom we have within, we can generate courage, hope, enthusiasm, confidence, trust, and faith to become limitless.

Specific goal-oriented affirmations are even more powerful and effective than simple affirmations. They are statements that describe your desires, or goals, as *already manifested*. They help you create the experience of already having manifested what you want. These affirmations create expectation; they give you motivation, and *Inspired Action* to act on your dreams.

Here is an example of a specific and goal-oriented affirmation:

-I am joyfully experiencing living in my beautiful beach front property on the island of Jamaica or something better.

- You must start your affirmations with the words *I am!* These two words are perhaps the two most powerful words in manifestation. The Subconscious mind interprets the *I am* as a command to make it happen.

- You must write your affirmations in the **present tense,** describing what you want as already manifested.

- You must state your affirmations in the **positive.** You must describe what you want, not what you don't want; this is because the Subconscious does not hear the word NO, DON'T, or NEVER. So, if you say, "I am not afraid of failure," the Subconscious hears it as, "I am afraid of failure." You must understand that the Subconscious only sees in pictures, not words, so the words, "I am not afraid," bring up a picture of being afraid. Also, you need to be aware of how you feel when you say or write your affirmations, If you are afraid of failure and you write, "I am not afraid of failure," your Subconscious mind not only sees this as, "I am afraid of failure," but now you have attached fear to it because you ARE afraid of failure. When you involve your emotions, you are adding so much more magnetic power to the attraction of what you want. So instead of saying, "I am not afraid of failure," say, "I am enjoying living a prosperous and successful life." Now, you begin to feel prosperous, and now you begin to feel good!

- You must keep your affirmations **Simple**.

- You must make your affirmations **Specific**.

- You must include an action word ending in – **ing**. Some examples of words are: experiencing, expressing, enjoying. Words ending in -*ing* help create the feeling as it is happening right now.

- You must include one word that adds **feeling or emotion** to your affirmation. Some examples of words are: Peacefully, happily, lovingly, joyfully.

- You can choose to add the words or **something better** at the very end of your affirmation. When you write your affirmations, and include the words "or something better", with no limitations, you can open the possibilities of receiving more if something better is available to you.

The best way to change your vibrational frequency to a feel-good or better one is to start with one simple affirmation, one simple word, then another, then another, until you feel unstoppable, invincible, transcendent, manifested! Only then you become! –Magie Cook

---

When you create your affirmations, it is best if you review them at least three times per day. The best times to review your affirmations are right before going to bed, when you awaken, and right after lunch. You listen to or read your affirmations right before you go to bed because that is the time when the brain goes into the sleep state; it is when it enters the Alpha level of the mind, which is the most receptive time for information to imprint into your Subconscious mind. It is also best to listen or read your affirmations right when you awaken because your mind is still at the Alpha level of receptivity, which allows for greater impact, and you also listen to your affirmations right after lunch, because you tend to feel a little sleepy or drowsy after eating a good meal, which makes it easier to enter into the Alpha level of mind.

When you read each affirmation, close your eyes and see yourself within your affirmation, visualize yourself in it. See yourself as you are living the experience you are describing in the present moment. Can you hear any sounds within your affirmation? For example, if you are at the beach, can hear the seagulls flying by, and the waves hitting the tide? Feel the feelings that you would feel as you have already achieved your success. Emotions are very powerful, so the stronger the emotions you feel, the stronger the attraction you will have to what you desire.

And the Lord answered me: "Write the vision; make it plain on tablets, so he may run who reads it. For still the vision awaits its appointed time; it hastens to the end-it will not lie. If it seems slow, wait for it; it will surely come; it will not delay. –Habakkuk 2:2-3

You can also practice writing your affirmations a few times per day. This will help them imprint with more power into the Subconscious mind. My favorite method of practicing the use of affirmations is when I record my affirmations into my smartphone. I then sit in front of a mirror, and as each affirmation comes up, I repeat it out loud and look at myself in the mirror. This method is very effective in surfacing the emotions for your deepest desires.

When I review my affirmations on a daily basis, I sometimes like to replace some action ending words or feeling words in my affirmations to keep them interesting and powerful. I want to be able to activate new and strong emotions every time I read them. I want to make sure that every time I read them; they create powerful feelings for me.

11

Mindful Meditations

There are different types of meditational programs available to you, based on the desired outcome that you wish to obtain. You can use meditation to pray, to find your center and connect to God, to un-clutter your mind and find inner peace, to clear and clean bad energies and blocks from your body, and so on. I have personally tried many types of success meditational programs, but never found a single program that truly unleashed the power of manifestation for me, until now. I created Mindful Meditations™ using MeditationCreator.com. I experienced the greatest success yet, in the application of it for my business.

MY GREATEST MIRACLE!

It all started when I decided that I wanted to increase my company sales and take my business to the next level. So, I sat down with a piece of paper and started to write a list of very powerful affirmations. Here are a few:

- I am a money magnet.

- Whatever I think about is being attracted to me.

- I am joyfully experiencing doing business with the largest supermarket in the US. They are going to contact me!

- I am joyfully experiencing standing in front of the buyer, and I am 100% prepared.

- With excitement, I open our products for testing, and the smell of fresh cut vegetables fills the room. Our products are the best tasting products they have ever tasted. I can see it on their faces.

- I gratefully shake hands with the buyer and obtain a supply contract.

When I wrote these affirmations, I wrote them in a way that I would be completely enveloped in them. I wanted to see myself in the place, I wanted to feel myself in the place, and I wanted to smell the smells in the place I was creating.

The next thing I did was to search online for meditational music that emotionally moved me the most, so that when I listened to it, my emotions would be deeply activated. I recorded my affirmations and my meditational music together, and I listened to them every morning right after waking up, and at night right before going to bed. I listened to them with full joy and conviction. When I listened to my recording, I used a hand placing technique that I created where I place my hands on different parts of my body, switching positions as I listened to each affirmation. This created an even deeper energetic and emotional feeling within me. This powerful technique made me feel as if I had already received what I was asking for. It was so amazing, and because I felt like I already had what I was asking for, I began being grateful that I had already received it. With gratitude, I created a very powerful and Spiritual vortex of attraction. I was creating a miracle!

On the twenty-ninth day, something unexpected happened. It was a Sunday and my business partner and I were sitting in my home discussing business for the following day when I got a phone call. The lady on the line said, "Hi, we were searching online looking for a salsa company to make a product for us. We searched ten companies and out of the ten, we thought that yours was the best." She said, "Are you interested in doing business with Wal- Mart?"

Every time I remember this event, I get chills all over my body! If you knew how the food retail business works, you would understand how difficult it is to get into Wal-

Mart. Still with disbelief, I said to her, "Is this a prank?" I couldn't believe it! My business partner couldn't believe it either! She asked that I proceed to ask for verification to see if they were legitimate.

We met with Wal-Mart almost immediately. The amazing thing for me was that meeting with the buyers happened just as I had visualized it. Wal-Mart took our products in and helped us surpass our first million dollars in business.

I created my miracle using the principle of autosuggestion with a combination of powerful affirmations and meditation, heightening my emotions created by the use of inspiring music, gratitude and my hand placing technique.

The most important factors in creating successful Mindful Meditations™ are to discover what your true desires are, release the things that are blocking you from obtaining them, along with other very important techniques. Because of my powerful manifestation experience, I was compelled to create Mindful Meditations™, and we now offer people the opportunity of creating their own personalized Mindful Meditations™ for their own success. (*To learn more about the hand placing technique visit our website at MagieCook.com*).

SUFFERING & RELEASING YOUR BREAKS

12

Personal Success Blocks

We all have experienced feeling stuck at one point in our lives, much like when you are driving a car with the emergency brake on and your foot on the gas pedal. The first step in releasing your brakes is *awareness*. To know that there is a reason you are feeling stuck and that you can do something about it. You must release your emotional brakes and limiting beliefs that are causing your suffering and keeping you from the life that you deserve, a life full of happiness and success.

The only one stopping you from success is YOU! Each and every one of us has experienced traumatic events throughout our lives. Every single event that ever happened in your lifetime is recorded in your Subconscious mind. These events don't even have to be traumatic; they can also be words someone spoke to you, something you witnessed, or a deeply rooted belief that you bought from someone. All of these events are stored within you as painful emotional memories. They are tucked away in your library of suffering, they are the things that are blocking you from your own personal success and happiness, from being completely free and full of love, and they may surface back into your life when something from the past triggers them back into your reality.

When you discover what the source of your limiting beliefs are, through your power of *awareness* you can begin to release them, and you can begin to *shift* them with the use of powerful life altering affirmations *(see Chapter 10 about Mindful Affirmations).*

When these painful emotional memories, limiting beliefs, and negative patterns surface back into your life, or when something from the past triggers them back into your reality, they happen in perfect timing. Why in perfect timing? Because there are no accidents, because you are ready to grow, you are ready to surface these painful memories and beliefs, and release them, because you are aware of what is happening and you are ready to love yourself; and the best thing you can give yourself is more love.

The truth is that *suffering begins in your mind*, and whether you are experiencing emotional or physical suffering, being aware of how you feel and doing something about it to release that suffering, is the greatest gift you can give yourself. Letting emotional pain build up within you can become so strong that, soon enough, it may eventually manifest in your life in many different ways. Sometimes emotional suffering can manifest in the form of a disease or as blocks preventing you from success; a feeling of being stuck, a constant reoccurring bad habit that you can't break, or simply fears that can cause many unfortunate events in your life.

Throughout his lifetime, Jose Silva, the world-renowned mind empowerment pioneer and psychology researcher, and the creator of the Silva Method, talked about how **90 percent of all illnesses are caused by the mind.** He also stated that if most illnesses were caused by the mind, it was extremely likely that most illnesses could be *reversed* by the mind as well.

The very first step to releasing your brakes is *awareness*. In order to truly break away from our painful emotional suffering, our limiting beliefs, and negative patterns, in order to truly release the shackles that keep us attracting the same undesired results into our lives, we must quiet our minds; we must go within and find out what those patterns are! You can begin by asking yourself,

-How is my relationship with myself?
-What is my current career situation?
-How is my love life?
-How is my financial situation?
-How is my health?
-How are my family relationships?

Or if you have a particular **reoccurring** problem that you are dealing with today you can begin by asking questions like:

-Why am I attracting the same negative circumstances in (my career, finances, health, business, family and relationships)?

-What are my beliefs about (my career, money, health, business, family and relationships)?

-What are my negative patterns about (my career, finances, health, business, family and relationships)?

If you feel discomfort when asking these questions, ask where the discomfort is coming from.

-Was it something my parents always said?

-Was it something I saw?

-Was it something I experienced?

If you are struggling in any of these areas, you are suffering from something that is blocking you from your freedom and happiness. To recognize what is blocking you, you must take 10-15 minutes of your time to quiet your mind and enter into meditation. Go within and ask your *higher self* to reveal to you the reasons behind what is blocking you from obtaining success. If at first you don't succeed, try this a couple of times, and passionately believe that you will receive the answers you are asking for. *(Visit MagieCook.com to learn about meditation)*. You must be still, and ask:

-*What is it that is* **blocking** *me from (being financially free, attracting my soul mate, starting a family, achieving perfect health)?*

Wait for your answers. Open your mind to review the events of your past that may have caused the emotional blocks you are suffering through. When you do this, have a pen and paper ready to write down the things that come up.

To begin *shifting* your *beliefs* and *releasing your brakes*, you can start by writing down your current limiting beliefs or emergency brakes in every area of your life (financial, career, business, health, family, relationships). You really start shifting your current limiting beliefs by writing a new belief right next to it, for example:

Current limiting belief/self-talk:

-*I can't generate enough money to feel financially free.*

New belief:

-There is more than enough money to go around. Everyone has the same access to unlimited riches.

If it becomes difficult for you to discover what is holding you back, or if you are dealing with issues that are deeply rooted and you are experiencing difficulty letting go, you may want to try the following techniques:

- The Emotional Freedom Technique at emofree.com
- The Work of Byron Katie at thework.com

I have found them to be tremendously effective in releasing negative beliefs, emotions, and thought patterns.

When you hold on to negative images and unhealthy beliefs that harbor your fears, guilt, and self-doubt, you suffer the effects of powerful experiences that you haven't released yet; you create your own personal blocks that keep you from attaining success in every area in your life.

If you are experiencing fear, you must understand that fear does not exist anywhere but in your mind. You must *remember who you really are!* The real you is beautiful, magnificent, transcendent, and a powerful Divine Being. Your eternal consciousness pervades your body and mind. The light of your true self is Pure Spirit, Source Energy, One with God, one with all that exists.

Nothing real can be threatened. Nothing Unreal exists. Herein lies the peace of God. –A Course in Miracles

In love and in harmony lies the peace of God. In Pure Spirit, there is no fear; in other words, in the presence of God, fear does not exist.

The next step for releasing your brakes is *forgiveness*. You will find that most of your blocks are related to something that someone said to you which impacted your life in a great way, something that someone did to you, or perhaps something that you saw with your eyes.

Something may have happened to you that caused you to doubt yourself, to think less of yourself, to feel unwanted, to feel guilty, to feel shame, to feel fear, or to feel unappreciated. Something made you feel unloved, and made you think that you will always have to struggle financially, and so forth. You must have the courage to surface these old negative emotions that have turned into your personal limiting beliefs and release them. You release all of the emotional poison and limiting beliefs through *forgiveness.*

You MUST *forgive yourself first*, forgive yourself for allowing your emotional poison to block, and rob you of your own happiness. You MUST then make it a point to reach out to all of those people who have affected you in a negative way. Forgive them and ask for forgiveness. Call them, talk to them, tell them how you feel, then release the emotional baggage that is holding you captive to them.

TOUGH LOVE

When I was young, I always told myself, "Love doesn't exist. Love is for weak people; I am tough." I was a tough tomboy who grew up in a family with over 200 kids in an orphanage, a place where I experienced constant fear, a place where I hardly ever got a hug or an "I love you" from my parents, because there were too many of us.

One of the things I will always remember was when I was 7 years old and got stung by a scorpion. I was in the mountains in Mexico, and I ran about a mile down to the house crying and told my dad, "Dad, I got stung by a scorpion." He looked at me with strong eyes and smacked me on the side of my head saying, "Shut up, Rambo, you are tougher than that!" I immediately stopped crying but kept sobbing. I was frightened because I saw many of his patients almost die of scorpion stings. I was afraid of dying, but I was made tough because I respected my father so much, and I looked up to him. The way I saw it was that there was no room for love; I had to be tough to survive.

There is one thing that I tried so hard to do with my father; I always tried to impress him in everything I did, but I never could. He never congratulated me, patted me on the back, or said, "Wow Magie, great job!" I wanted to be recognized for my hard work and, because I wasn't, I always worked harder and harder, hoping to get something out of him. I did it because I looked up to him so much, and I wanted to be like him: strong, admired, and respected. Whether it was cutting trees in the forest with my brothers and carrying them down to the house on my shoulder, carrying 60-pound bags of dirt from the mountains for planting my mother's plants, building barbed wire fences, or digging ditches, I always got his jobs done far more quicker than most of the boys. Many years later, one of my older adoptive brothers came to visit me here in the US. We sat down to talk about our past experiences living at the orphanage; we laughed and cried all at the same time. When we talked about this experience and how much it bothered me, he said to me, "No, Magie, listen to me. We all knew you were better than a lot of us in doing every task. The reason he didn't recognize your success was because we were in the group with you. You were his biological daughter, and he didn't want to give you all of the attention and recognition in front of us. He didn't want us to feel bad. He wanted to treat us all the same, whether adopted or biological. He didn't want to show any preference, in order to prevent hurting the other kids' feelings about not being wanted, knowing where they came from." He said, "He looked up to you, he told me." Wow, it made sense! I was in tears again!

I always thought that I wished I had grown up in a normal family, in an environment where I got lots of hugs and "I love you" from my parents. But the truth is that there are no accidents! Everything that has happened in my life has shaped me to be the person I am today, and that is perfect in all nature! There are no regrets.

FORGIVENESS & LOVE

I sat down to meditate one afternoon, and I was asking for guidance towards forgiveness, looking into every bad memory I had with my father. I wanted to clear my spirit of any negative energy, and I was working on releasing my personal blocks. When I was meditating, the first thing that came to me as a bad feeling was the fact that I felt neglected. When I felt this deep into my meditation, a strong voice spoke to me, sending chills down my spine. It said, "Remember when I used to ask you to sit beside me at my clinic on Sundays while I gave medical attention to the poor?" I clearly remembered those times. I remember he would send one of the kids for me every Sunday, and I sat on a wooden chair next to him thinking, "I want to play! I want to be with the other kids playing right now!" Then the voice spoke to me again saying, "All I wanted was for you to be in my presence, and I wanted to feel yours." I opened my eyes from the meditation and began to cry! I realized this was God speaking to me on behalf of my father. See, God is always with us; he never leaves. We will wander through life thinking we are alone, but we are not! All you have to do is feel his presence. Feeling the power of God's presence in your life is having awareness. It is far more powerful than words, hugs, or "I love you." You become alive in him and through him! This message was life changing for me. All those years I didn't understand why my father had me sit on a wooden chair next to him every Sunday, but I finally understood why he did it. He just wanted to feel my presence. It was his way of spending time with me. I just wasn't aware. In that moment, I forgave my father for every bad memory and feeling of neglect!

Throughout my childhood life I had a tremendous amount of resentment towards my mother. I never agreed with the rough methods she used to discipline us.

Because of what I lived and experienced, one of my greatest emotional battles happened in my dreams. I had recurring nightmares that lasted for years, until the age of 21. I would wake up in the middle of the night shouting and crying. I would dream that my mother was chasing me with an electrical cable in her hand to punish me with, I was running down a hill, and I was desperately in panic. All of a sudden, I would take off flying. I felt instant relief! I barely made it! I could fly! Away in the mountains, I would wait for a few days being watchful, then I would come back when my parents were not around and teach my brothers and sisters how to fly so they could fly away with me. The worst part of my dream was that I wanted to save everyone, and my biggest fear was that I wouldn't be able to. In my dream, I only had the ability to save 3 or 4 of my siblings, and the rest stayed behind in suffering and, eventually, death.

One summer afternoon, several years later, one of my mother's sisters contacted me over the Internet. We started to talk about my mother's family and her past. On our recorded conversations, she began to reveal to me how my mother was kept like a slave in her home and how she never grew up like a normal kid. She was told that she would stay with her parents to care for them until they passed. There was incest in her family, and she lived through a lot of suffering.

I immediately broke down into tears! I thought to myself, "I believe that I finally understand where my mother came from and the suffering she endured." That explained everything! In that moment, I forgave her for the deep resentment I had towards her all of my life!

The next day, I asked my father if he would let her come visit me for one week, and to my surprise, he did! A few days later, when I drove up to the airport to pick her up, I was very nervous. It was as if I was meeting her for the very first time. As I drove up to the main entrance, I saw her outside the door standing in a humble pose, and I immediately felt an overwhelming feeling of restraint overcoming my body. I felt like there was a knot in my stomach. When I got out of my car, it was as if I could barely open my arms and tell her, "I love you," for the first time. We spent the best week of our lives together. We went shopping everywhere; I took her to get her very first full body massage, and a chocolate facial because she loves chocolate, and we did so many more amazing things together that week.

At the end of the week before my mother went back to Mexico, we were sitting at a restaurant having breakfast and my mother said to me, "Magie, you have changed... why you are so different with me now? You have never been like this with me before." When I looked at her, I was immediately filled with emotions, and I wanted to burst out crying but I held it together. I wanted to tell her that I knew everything about her life in the past, and that I wanted to forgive her, but I couldn't tell her.

It wasn't until ten years later that I understood the real power of emotions and how the past had been keeping me from my own happiness and greater success.

I lost my home and the person I loved and cared for the most. My business wasn't doing very well, and many other strong and undesired things were manifesting into my life. I had the realization of how blocked I was because of my past experiences. I had the feeling that my suffering, and my block, was in connection to my mother. It was then that I had the courage to call my mother and ask her for forgiveness.

I picked up the phone and said, "Mom, remember that week 10 years ago when you came to visit me, and you asked me why I was so different towards you when we were sitting in that restaurant?" She said, "Yes." I said, "It's because I found out about your past, how you were kept like a slave and how there was incest in your family, but I couldn't tell you that I knew. It was too powerful, and I didn't know what to expect from you." I finally understood you, and I forgave you for everything. But this time I want you to know that I know what happened to you and that I understand you. I would like to ask for your forgiveness for all of the resentment I held against you." I can't believe I bottled this suffering within me for so long.

After a very long and great conversation with my mother, she proceeded to ask me for forgiveness as well. She said to me, "Magie, all the children we took in all those years came in with tremendous emotional problems, and did terrible things, and the way we disciplined everyone to try to fix the problems was not right. Your father and I were overwhelmed. I feel like you guys are all traumatized." When she said this, I remembered how my father used to say that all of us were brain damaged." My mother then proceeded to say "I have found through many years that the best way to treat the children is with LOVE not punishment. Will you forgive me?" I immediately broke into tears. I said, "YES, I love you very much!" I was astonished by my mother's realization of using LOVE to deal with the children's problems. This truly filled my entire being with joy. Joy that you cannot even begin to understand! At that moment, I was set free! Free of bondage from the terrible memories, nightmares, and emotions from the past.

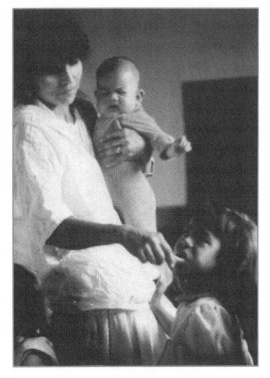

My mother was always trying to do her best in taking care of all of my brothers and sisters. She was always doing so many things at the same time. I still don't know how she did it!

After speaking with my mother, I began writing letters and picking up the phone, calling everyone I could think of who had made a negative impact on my life. I asked everyone for forgiveness, and I was forgiven. I told everyone how much I loved them, and I couldn't wait to see them in person to tell them face to face and to give them a hug. I also asked them to share their favorite memory of us and I would do the same to focus on and share the best things of the past.

My decision and courage to ask for forgiveness and receive it felt a huge weight that came off of my shoulders. I literally felt like I was floating! I looked at myself in the mirror. My cheeks were rosy, and my eyes were wide open. I felt free! I felt complete love and happiness. I began to see everyone with love. My world had changed! My shackles were off!

The thing to remember about *forgiveness* is that when you forgive someone, or ask for forgiveness, you must not keep it to yourself; they must know that you are asking for forgiveness, they must acknowledge your need for forgiveness. This really helps you deal with letting things go. This is very helpful in releasing your negative feelings, because you want to be heard, you want things to be known. This is the first step in truly releasing the blocks that are holding you back. My mother needed to know what I knew about her, she needed to know how I felt about her, and she needed to know how she had impacted my life. *My forgiveness became the acceptance of her, and her forgiveness became the acceptance of me*, the release of the negative emotions I had towards her and the release of the negative emotions she had towards me.

Forgiveness is energy that connects us. It must be released both ways. There must be healing both ways. If forgiveness is not released both ways, then it becomes a problem only for the person withholding forgiveness. It no longer affects you because you have asked for forgiveness, and God always forgives. You let them know that you have made a choice to release the bondage between the two of you. Then you will no longer be affected.

ACCEPTANCE

I visited my family one summer in Mexico, and as soon as we drove into the gates of the ranch I got out of the car, and all of my siblings ran to greet me with hugs, but for some reason, my eyes were fixed on one of my older adopted sisters. Her facial expression looked like she was about to burst into tears. I felt compelled to walk directly to her to hug her; she sighed, and her body caved into my arms as she began to cry. I had no idea what was going on in her life, but I told her, "You are stronger than you think, you are a superhero." I knew she was a runaway and was heavily involved in prostitution. I knew she was suffering, and she wanted relief. It was not until I had come back to the States that she contacted me and told me, "Magie, your hug and words relieved me! My biggest problem is that I feel so bad! I feel so bad because my mother had told me that the reason Dad died was because of me."

Her father's death had nothing to do with her. He suffered a heart attack while preaching in one of the villages in rural Mexico. He passed away doing what he loved. What a tremendous burden to put on someone! Her mother had clearly transferred all of her emotional poison to her and she received it with wide open arms. Her mother practically said, "Here, I give you this poison; receive it, it's toxic, you should feel bad because I feel bad. I want to share with you the fact that I feel bad," and she received it fully and completely. She was scarred by it! It gave her an emotional wound that could possibly take a lifetime to heal! Just because someone gives us emotional poison does not mean we have to take it. You need to understand that the real problem lies with the person giving it. They are affected by their own emotional poison and they want to give it to someone else, hoping it will make them feel better, but it only makes them feel worse. If someone tries to give you their emotional poison, you simply understand that what they are going through is their problem and not yours, and because you choose not to take anything personally, you truly love yourself unconditionally. This is very powerful! If they keep trying to give you their emotional poison, you say to them with love that what they are trying to do does not affect you, because it is not your problem, and that you love them very much. As soon as this happens, they will no longer try to give you their poison because they have completely lost power over you. Now they know that they won't waste their breath giving you any more emotional poison, because it does not affect you. They know that they can't get the reaction they expect from you anymore, because you love yourself so much that your shield of self-love is protecting you.

When I was told by my father that I would not amount to anything, that I would die in prison and with AIDS, I never forgot his words because they were very impacting to me, but I chose not to believe him. I made a decision not to take his words personally, and I also made a choice that day to prove to myself that he was wrong, that I was very special and worthy of wonderful and great things in life as an LGBT woman. He obviously had a problem when he said those words, a problem that I was not going to allow to enter my world. Perhaps if I would have chosen to listen to his words and receive his emotional poison, I would not have created my successes, built a multimillion-dollar business, or be sitting here writing a book about success and transformation.

When you truly love yourself unconditionally, you **accept** who you are fully and completely with all of your imperfections, and you always remember *who you really are* as an amazing Divine Spiritual being. What other people say about you does not bother you, you don't take what they say personally, you let go of your fears and begin to feel loved, healthy, beautiful, abundant, and prosperous, regardless of any circumstances. You realize that there is no one else out there like you, that you are perfect just as you are, with every scar and defect. When you can love yourself completely and unconditionally, your love starts flowing outwards. Instead of needing someone else's love or approval, you have plenty of love to give, you approve of yourself, and you magically begin attracting the success you want in your life.

Let every action, every reaction, every thought and every emotion be based on love. Increase your self-love until the entire dream of your life is transformed from fear and drama to love and joy. —The Mastery of Love

---

One of my younger sisters contacted me in distress. She had found out that our mother had said something to the family about her past that no one knew, and this really tore her apart. She was in tears when she spoke to me about it, since this really bothered her. I asked her to quiet her mind and write down everything she felt towards our mother with the emotions she was feeling. She wrote, "My mother disappoints me, she does not respect me because she is involved in my personal life and that causes me pain. She makes me feel angry because she is judging me again and pulling the blood between us apart. I have tried to love her and get along with her. I feel better realizing that I don't have a mother. She is always crushing me. She could be using me as an example for being accomplished in my career and being independent." She kept going on and on.

So, I picked out simple statements from her long message and put them on paper:

-I am disappointed with Mom.

-Mom doesn't respect me.

-Mom causes me pain from the past.

-Mom makes me feel angry.

-Mom judges me.

-Mom is pulling us apart.

-Mom is crushing me.

-I realized my Mom has always been like that.

I then asked her to take these statements and turn them around to herself. This is what they read:

-I am disappointed with myself.

-I don't respect myself.

-I cause myself pain from the past.

-I make myself feel angry.

-I judge myself.

-I am pulling us apart.

-I am crushing myself.

-I realized I have always been like that.

This helped her realize that the problem was not with our mother but with herself. This was her realization, her Acceptance. She was the one feeling these things and creating this emotional poison with her thoughts, causing her to deeply suffer. This allowed her to forgive herself first, then talk to her mother about it and forgive her, too.

As I began living my turnarounds, I noticed that **I was everything I called you.** *You were merely my projection. Now, instead of trying to change the world around me (this didn't work, but only for 43 years), I can put the thoughts on paper, investigate them, turn them around, and find that I am the very thing I thought you were. In the moment I see you as selfish, I am selfish (deciding how you should be). In the moment I see you as unkind, I am unkind. If I believe you should stop waging war, I am waging war on* you *in my mind.*
— *Byron Katie*

Remember that when something bothers you about someone else, it is not their problem, it is yours. It is something that is bothering you, not them. It could be something that was triggered from a thought or belief you hold in your Subconscious from the past. It becomes an emotional pain, a poison, and a block. That is why, when someone yells at you, or says or does something terrible to you, it has nothing to do with you, and everything to do with them, it is a problem they have. This is where you learn not to take things personally, and you completely understand why. This is when you don't allow someone else's emotional poison to infect your wellbeing. This poison is like a disease that spreads, and it may in fact turn into a disease in your body, depending on how it is received and handled by your mind.

Acceptance becomes a success when you accept others for who they are with all of their imperfections, and regardless of whatever may have happened in the past between you and them because you have chosen to forgive them. *Acceptance* comes when you let people be who they are, without trying to control or change them. *Acceptance* is realizing that who they are does not have a negative effect on you because you are responsible for your own happiness, not them. I have always said that we are all perfectly flawed. We all have our faults, we all make mistakes, but they are perfect because they make us who we are, when we choose to learn and grow from them.

13
Hereditary Success Blocks

I later discovered how one single event from the past, a conversation, or memory filled with *emotional poison* can completely block us from success. But listen to this...this is not coming from you but coming from your loved ones! A block will pop into our lives when we least expect it and manifest itself in the form of fear or in the feeling of being stuck.

"Our fathers have sinned and are not; and we have borne (been punished for) their iniquities." Lamentations 5:7

This is a Spiritual bondage that is passed from one generation to the next. They are continual negative patterns passed down, not because we were around our birth parents to learn how they behaved, but because we inherited their Spiritual bondage. This is way beyond learned behavior.

Some examples of this are mental problems, persistent fears that are not rational, depression, continual financial difficulties, and even illnesses! Basically, anything that seems to be a persistent struggle may well be a generational Spiritual Bondage.

Jeremiah makes it clear that believers are redeemed from generational curses in Jeremiah 31:29-30, but in the next chapter he clearly says, "You show love to thousands but bring the punishment for the parents' sins into the laps of their children after them." (Jeremiah 32:18)

In the story of Mark 9:17-27, Jesus deals with what is almost certainly a generational Spiritual bondage. A man brought his son to Jesus. He told Jesus that his son was possessed by a spirit that had robbed him of speech. Whenever the spirit would seize him, it would throw him on the ground, sometimes in the fire or water to try to kill him. He would foam from the mouth and his teeth would clench, his jaw becoming rigid.

Jesus asked the boy's father how long he had been like that, and his father replied, "from childhood". When the boy's father desperately tells Jesus, "If you can do anything, take pity on us, help us," Jesus says to him, "...if you can? Everything is possible for one who believes" (verse 23). Immediately the boy's father said, "I do believe; help me overcome my unbelief!" Jesus then rebuked the impure spirit, commanded it to come out of him and never to enter him again.

In this story you can clearly see that Jesus didn't ask the boy one single question, he spoke entirely with his father, where the generational Spiritual bondage came from, and that is how he became liberated; because Jesus understood where this bondage was coming from.

"And you can break yourself free from your hereditary patterns, cultural codes, social beliefs; and prove once and for all that the power within you is greater than the power that's in the world" —Michael Bernard Beckwith

My mother once told me something that was very emotionally impacting to me, something that completely awakened my awareness to forgive and release a tremendous block for myself and my entire family! It was a curse. Her father had said that all of his twelve kids would be affected by the Garcia curse! For several years before his passing, her father lived locked in his room in complete darkness. Through the years I had seen several of my family members suffer from Spiritual torment, emotional instability, and reoccurring problems in almost every area in their lives. If you are a member of the Garcia family and you are reading this book, I invite you to go within right now and ask God to release all Spiritual bondage! Be free, now! Forgive and receive forgiveness, accept and receive acceptance. Even though my grandfather has passed, I choose to forgive him, and I also completely love and accept him!

If you are suffering from reoccurring negative patterns in your life, you are more likely suffering from a hereditary Spiritual bondage. You have a choice to break yourself free. You can do it TODAY!

EMOTIONAL POISON

When I started my inspirational business, I started to feel like something was not right, and for some reason I felt a tremendous lack of self-worth; I had a block, and I had no idea where it was coming from. So, I set time aside for meditation and I discovered that there was something that was still creating a block between my mother and me. I contacted her and told her how I was feeling like there was an energy block between us. She could not think of anything until I asked her if she could think of something that may have happened when I was in her womb, something that perhaps got directly transferred to me from her. At this point, she got very emotional! This was the only time I had ever heard my mother cry, and when she began to cry, I began to cry because I know how strong my mother is!

She proceeded to tell me that when she was pregnant with me, she almost died! She said that she was in the hospital bed when my father grabbed the phone to call her parents.

See, my mother's parents are from a strong Navajo Indian descent, and my father was white. My mother's parents always said that, in their family, none of their kids were allowed to marry white men or women. When my father had a calling to go to Mexico, to take over an orphanage to prevent 36 kids from going into the streets because his dear friend had passed away, he asked my mother to come with him, and so she did. My mother and father were no longer welcomed in my mother's home in Albuquerque, NM.

So, my father contacted my mother's parents at the hospital and asked them if they wished to talk to my mother. He said, "Do you wish to talk with Lucia? This may be the last time you get to talk to her; she has typhoid fever and may not be able to come out alive." Their response was, "We don't have a daughter named Lucia," and they hung up the phone. My mother was in the lowest possible place in her life with me in the womb, and at the same time she received the worst emotional poison from the people she loved the most.

*I can't even imagine how she felt! And she was transferring all that emotional poison to me, which later manifested as a **lack of self-worth** block in my life. My mother said, "I need to call my mom and talk to her! Ask for forgiveness!" She needed to release this thing that was connecting us all into a block. I told my mother, "Mom, the most important thing that you need to know right now is to remember **who you really are**!" I told her something very beautiful I read in an empowering Spiritual book once. I said to her, "You are a beautiful divine being, whose eternal consciousness pervades your body and mind, and is the light of your true self shining across to mine; I bow to that transcendent being that is also the real you. I love you." I said to her, "Mom, your true family, your true father is the Father that lives within you that also lives in me, it is also The Spirit of God, it is also the ONENESS that exists in all that is, and he never abandons us." She told me no one had ever told her something so true, something so beautiful!*

14

Gratitude

It is very important to maintain an attitude of gratitude. Two of the most powerful words that you could say are, *"Thank You."* You may not know this, but *Gratitude* is indeed a secret to success. Being in a state of appreciation is powerful in manifesting your desires.

I often find myself driving my car, and as I start to tear up a little, I grip the steering wheel tightly; I start looking around, admiring my car and all the things in it. I think, "Wow, I have a car. I love this car; I never owned a car in Mexico. Thank you!"

This is so powerful because *your focus is in this*

moment, you are in *appreciation* of what you currently have, and when you are in the state of appreciation of what you currently have, you are activating one of the most powerful laws of the Universe, *The Law of Attraction*, bringing more of what you want into your life. The Law of Attraction says that like attracts like, and because you are focusing on what you have received, instead of focusing on what you don't have, you always get more of what you focus your attention to.

When you remember to have an *attitude of Gratitude*, you are living in the state of the *highest emotional vibrations possible*. Gratitude is Love, because it is an emotional expression of feeling complete about something that you have already received; Gratitude is Joy, because you are experiencing the thrill of living in the moment with the understanding that you are attracting more things to be Grateful for, Gratitude is Peace, because it is already there, you are holding it, and it is done. To vibrate in the frequencies of Love, Joy, and Peace is to vibrate in the highest vibrations possible for attracting your desires (peace being the highest frequency you can have). To vibrate in the frequencies of guilt and shame is to vibrate in the lowest frequencies that humanly exist.

Have you ever noticed that when you give a gift to someone and they show so much Gratitude and appreciation, you just want to continue to give them more? This is how The Law of Attraction works, both in the interpersonal and Universal Spiritual levels of manifestation.

My favorite moments to be Grateful for during the day are when I think about something profound that has affected my life in a positive way; I get so filled with emotion that no matter where I am or what I am doing, I will stop and kneel on one leg or put my hands together in the prayer position in appreciation. This always brings tears to my eyes. I am in a state of complete love, joy, and appreciation.

There are many different things you can choose from to apply Gratitude into your life. For example, you can use Gratitude when remembering your past successes and the times when you have triumphed. When you do this, you are not only attracting more success to you, but you are birthing a fire of desire to act and do more, based on inspiration. It is very important to remember your successes and remember to be Grateful for them. The best way to remember your successes is to display your accomplishments, trophies, newspaper articles, and awards in a visible place in your home or office. You can also create a *Daily Victory Log* where you record all of your accomplishments.

ACKNOWLEDGING PAST SUCCESSES

Acknowledging your past successes is inspiration that breeds a fire in you for attaining your future goals, it also gives you *Inspired Action* and opens the doorway to experiencing more of what you want in your life.

I sat down with my team in a morning meeting to discuss the manufacturing plans for the day, but before we got started, I asked them to write on a piece of paper all of the successes they could think of from their past. One of my team members sat in his chair with a look of disappointment on his face, and he proceeded to say, "I don't have any successes in my life." I looked at him and said, "Tom, do you realize that you being here this very morning is an accomplishment?" He looked at me and smiled, and then started writing.

Success, whether you consider it to be big or small, is an accomplishment that moves you forward, and gives you a reason for living; it gives you joy, but you need to acknowledge it, embrace it, thank yourself for it, and reward yourself for it.

If you *choose* to turn every accomplishment each day into a recognizable success, you will feel empowered. You will feel like you want to do more, because you want to feel more amazing. You become a winner and a superhero; you become unstoppable, and your so-called problems that comes your way are no longer seen as problems, you see these events as opportunities to grow and expand, to become better, wiser, happier, and richer. You ask yourself, "What is the seed in this that is meant to teach me something or make me better?" You change the way you look at things, because you understand that if you change the way you look at things, the things you look at change.

One *very* powerful technique that you can start practicing today is to *start being Grateful for the things you haven't manifested yet.* When you are being grateful for the things you haven manifested yet, you are tricking your Subconscious mind into thinking that you already have what you are asking for. Remember that your Subconscious does not know right from wrong, good from bad, it just does as commanded by the Conscious mind.

A very powerful technique that you can use to add a tremendous amount of influence to your future manifestations is to combine Affirmations with Gratitude. Because of the tremendous energetical power of attraction in Gratitude, Affirmations become even more powerful when you combine them together.

You can begin your affirmations like this:

-I am so Grateful and Thankful now that ...

This process is even more exhilarating when you use the hand placing technique I use *(visit* MeditationCreator.com *for more information on the hand placing technique).*

You also add more power to your Gratitude Affirmations when you repeat them to yourself as often as you can, but this process must feel good. When you do this, you are using the principle of Autosuggestion, which is imprinting the powerful message to your Subconscious mind. The more you repeat the message, pretty soon the Subconscious mind believes your message to be true; it will accept it as true, and therefore it will say, "It is done," and this is when manifestation happens. This is so much fun.

For example, if you are having trouble with lack of self-esteem because of your weight, you can write a gratitude affirmation that says :

-I am so Grateful and Thankful now that I am joyfully experiencing my perfect weight at 125 lbs or something better.

You effortlessly achieve your perfect weight because of the powerful effect that Gratitude Affirmations have, they help you stay focused and Grateful for being in your perfect weight, *in this moment, now*! Now every time you eat and exercise, you remember to say your Gratitude Affirmation, and you start believing your message the more you say it. You become aware of your eating habits and the way you exercise. Because you are focused on your message, you are inspired by it. Not only is The Law of Attraction working in your favor, but now you have opened the possibilities for even better things to manifest because you added the words *'or something better'* to the end of your statement. With the words 'or something better' you are opening yourself to the unlimited possibilities that exist in the Universe, you are asking the Universe to manifest for you something even better if it is available. Soon enough, you are sporting your wonderful beautiful body and your self-esteem is bliss.

REMEMBER WHERE YOU CAME FROM

One of my most inspiring and altering moments that brings me such Joy, Love, and Appreciation is when I take the time to remember where I came from, and where I am today.

The biggest impact on me out of all of my childhood experiences was the time we lived in poverty, especially in my younger years. Growing up in a Mexican orphanage with over 200 kids was very tough for the financial wellbeing of my family. My parents did not get any financial help from the Mexican government. We depended on monetary donations that came from friends, churches, and supporters from the United States. Every Thursday, my father would drive two hours to the nearest town, called Morelia, to pick up what he called, "The package". It was a large-sized DHL envelope containing multiple letters with money contributions for their non-profit organization. This was the happiest day of the week for my father. Every Thursday, he would dance like a kid when he received the package. This is when he received money to buy the things we needed to survive, but money always brought conflict in the household. My father's heart was always filled with deep compassion for the poor because he was deeply connected to their suffering; most of the time, he gave away all the money that came in. As a result, we would go sometimes two to three weeks without food. At times, my siblings and I didn't have shoes and our clothes always had holes in them. I remember making my own shoes out of pieces of tire rubber and cutting out strings from cow skin in the leather shop my dad had by the barns. I will always remember what it feels like to be hungry. My mother always argued with my father, "You need to feed our kids first! They need food, shoes, and clothes. We never have enough money to survive!"

When my siblings and I were in Elementary school, our teachers desperately asked my father to buy us black shoes for the school attire, because we didn't have any. They had told him that if we didn't have black shoes, we would not be accepted in that school. My father had very little money, and with it he bought everyone the cheapest sandals and pairs of socks he could find, and he painted our feet with black tar (the stuff they use for highway roads). Our teachers were very disappointed with my father about that, but my father loved it.

When we had animals, my mother delegated to me all of the animal killings for food. No one did it better than I did. I was so good at it that I became a hunter in the mountains of Mexico. When I was older and we would get hungry, a few of my brothers and I would get lost in the mountains, and we hunted different animals for food with our bare hands and only a knife.

My original hunting knife

At night, we took turns sleeping in trees. We had to pick certain branches to sleep in, to make sure we didn't fall during the night. When we saw our prey, we communicated with noises, put a spotlight in the face of the animal to neutralize it, then jump on it to capture it. We would skin the animal, clean it up by the river, and cook it right then and there. This was so much fun!

I am also very grateful for discipline. Discipline has given me tremendous success in life. Growing up in the orphanage, we had to be very disciplined in order to keep everything running smoothly, and to keep everything organized. I remember my father made us march like soldiers in straight lines on our way to the dining room every day. The dining room had very long tables, and all the tables had our names on them, so everyone was designated a spot to eat. Everyone had a spoon, a cup, and a plate with our names marked on them.

One of three tables where we sat down to eat our meals.
The tub on the table was always filled with jalapenos.

When it was time to eat, we would bless the food, then get in a line to get our food.

My siblings serving each other food

When we were done eating, we would get in a line to wash our spoon, cup, and plate, and then they were returned to our spots with our names on them. My mother always delegated chores and we did everything in teams. Cooking and cleaning were broken into teams, one week the girls would cook, and the boys would clean, and the next the boys would cook, and the girls would clean. This would sometimes turn into a competition.

Every morning we would wake up at around 4 am to cook breakfast and prepare lunch for the kids going to school in town, and for the kids that were home-schooled as well. We had to hand cut and cook 50-pound bags of potatoes, and other vegetables in big pans. I would get up with my brothers sometimes to go looking for our cows in *the mountains. We would guide them back into the barn to milk them so we would have fresh warm milk for breakfast.*

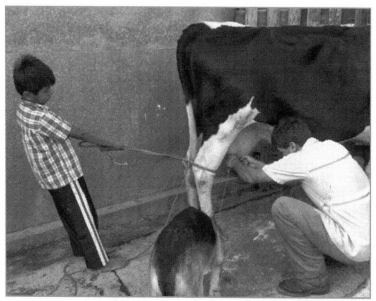

My adopted brothers Joel and Fernando preparing the cow to be milked for breakfast

Sometimes it was so dark that you would run into one. We had to be very careful with the bulls; it was very easy for them to get angry. I have a scar on my leg as a reminder of how stubborn they were. I got chased by a bull one morning because one of my brothers was making a noise that made him angry. I was the first one he saw, and he started chasing after me. I jumped the barbed wire fence and barely made it, but I slashed my leg open with a barb.

Our dorms had bunk beds in them, and they had to be kept very clean and well organized.

When some of us had beds, the frames were made of metal and the bed itself was made out of wood planks. We didn't have mattresses, only a blanket to cover ourselves with.

All the kids, starting from the age of four, had to hand wash their own clothes each day. Before we had a Laundromat with washboards, we washed our clothes in the river or on the driveway. My mother was very strict about washing our clothes clean. If she found one single spot on them, we had to go back and wash them again. It was very easy to rip holes into them. If you didn't wash your clothes, you got disciplined for it. For each garment you had, you got five spankings bent over on bare skin. If you put your hands between you and the stick, trying to cover up from the spanking, it didn't count.

This photo was taken before we had a laundromat. Here you see my adopted sister Nancy washing her clothes on the driveway.

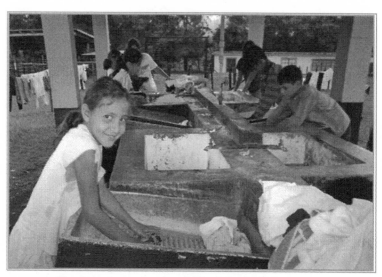

The laundromat my parents later built for us

If you needed to go to the bathroom, my mom would give you one square of toilet paper for #1 and two squares of toilet paper for #2. We also had to conserve as much as we could.

When I think about who I was then and who I am now, I am filled with so much tremendous emotional Gratitude that it overpowers my entire being. I never thought that I would be here today, a beautiful, strong, successful woman, with so many accomplishments, writing this book to share my inspiring experiences with you.

The most important thing that you can do for yourself each day is to form a habit of being Grateful. I figured out a way to remind myself to practice being Grateful and staying inspired each day.

I created the "I AM" project. It is physical reminder – a bracelet – that helps you stay centered. You can use it creatively in many ways. I use it to declare your power and divinity by practicing the art of manifestation. This bracelet is so effective for me because it helps me remember me who I really am and the mentality I want to maintain during the course of my busy day. You can learn more about this product at MagieCook.com.

Every person is unique and different, every day you feel different; your desires change, you want to feel good, and new desires always come up. I wear my bracelet on my right hand and every time I look down during the course of the day, it brings a smile to my face. When I see it, it reminds me to stay grateful and inspired about my message.

MAGIE COOK

15
Your Health & Success

It is imperative that you understand how important being healthy is for your overall success. Your heath has a great impact on every area of your life. When you are healthy you feel good, you feel energized, and you feel strong; therefore, your mental attitude is strong, energized, and it feels inexhaustible. By taking care of your body, you are honoring your mind and Spirit. When you raise your energy levels through mindful eating and exercising, you are putting out a much stronger attraction signal to all of your future life's manifestations. When you increase your energy levels,

MAGIE COOK

your attraction power to manifest your desires also increases.

Being healthy is a state of mind, just like anything else that you purposefully focus on. The more you focus on any single thing in your life, the more power you add to that specific thing, creating miraculous results. You must understand that focus needs to have *awareness* and *purpose*. Be Aware that your focus is free of misconceptions or hidden negative beliefs that you have created about yourself through your life. Set time aside to meditate and quiet your mind. Ask yourself if there is anything within you that is stopping you from accomplishing a healthy state of being; if there is anything that you were told, anything that you saw, or anything you may have heard from someone else that is deeply rooted within you. Once you figure out what is holding you back, you will be able to release it. Releasing these negative beliefs about your healthy wellbeing will unlock the success that you need to achieve the results you passionately seek. Once you release your old limiting beliefs, you can begin to reprogram your Subconscious mind with life-altering Affirmations *(refer to Chapter 12 to read about Personal*

216

Success Blocks, and Chapter 11 to read about Mindful Affirmations).

When I was growing up, I often saw my father gain and lose a lot of weight in a short period of time. He would eat large amounts of foods very quickly, and when he talked about being overweight it impacted my life, so I became just like him. Another thing that greatly impacted my health was growing up in an orphanage where, many times, we didn't have food, and when we had it, it was not always tasty. I can remember eating mostly whole vegetables cooked in water, sometimes with no salt, and foods like beans and rice that were sometimes burned and with no taste as well.

Sometimes my mother took the time out of her busy schedule to cook a special dinner for all of us, and these were very delicious! When we had these dinners, we would eat them so fast, and without enjoying them because we were afraid that the food was going to run out, or we were afraid someone was going to take it from us.

When I came to America, I discovered food and its amazing flavors. When I sat down to eat, I would eat a lot of it very quickly. I realized I was repeating one of my childhood's negative eating patterns. I did this so automatically, and without even thinking about it. When I started being mindful about eating great foods, I changed my beliefs to:

-There is more than enough of food to go around.

-I am enjoying every bite of food I take and its great satisfying taste.

-I feel great about everything I eat, and I bless it for the vitality of my body.

Yes, what you eat has a great impact on your weight status. So, if you find yourself having a few or more extra pounds, understand that what you are today is the result of what you have been *eating, thinking,* and *feeling* in the past, and only you have the power to change your current manifestation. You may think that you need to starve to lose a few or more pounds, but that is wrongful thinking. Choosing healthy foods and eating the right portions through the day is not only the result of my perfect weight, but it's also the feelings and emotions you are having while eating your foods that has an impact on your overall weight status.

If you crave ice cream, a good piece of your favorite cake or pie, or anything else that you have a weakness for, go for it! But when you do, be 100% *mindfully aware* of the deliciousness of it, and enjoy it to the fullest. You Never sacrifice anything you like. When you sacrifice something that you truly love, the craving for it builds up so much that at some point you can't contain yourself and you end up overindulging, and afterwards feeling extremely guilty about it. When you are mindfully aware of what you are eating, you find that you are completely satisfied with less, and you feel great! When you are mindfully aware of what you are eating, you are focusing on abundant health, you are focusing on feeling good about being in your perfect weight, you are completely in the moment. Instead of having fear about gaining weight, you become joyful about being in your perfect weight, and you do this because you understand how your mind works in relationship with your thoughts, emotions, and feelings. You understand that what you think about, you bring about. If you constantly feel or think "I am going to be overweight" while you are eating your foods, then you will attract being more overweight.

ENJOY NOW!

I visited one of my sisters one Christmas and she cooked this great, amazing meal. I sat at the table and watched her eat. She looked very depressed as she began eating the delicious food she had just prepared for all of us. She had a frown on her face, and her body was slouching to one side. I asked her, "Why do you look so sad?" She replied, "Because when I am done eating this amazing food, it's all going to be gone, and I will no longer taste the goodness of it." She was focusing on how she would feel after she was done eating her food instead of enjoying every bite of it, instead of enjoying the moment of having it now. As a result, she had been overweight because every time she would eat, she ate so much, having the same feelings of not having enough satisfaction. Wow! She was creating complete suffering within herself by repeating this behavior and state of mind every single time she ate. She was in her own mental prison, filled with negative beliefs and affirmations. I can't even begin to tell you how many times she passionately and desperately stated with a lot of emotion, "Magie, I am so overweight," throughout the day!

The truth is that within our conscious self-talk, each and every one of us does this repeatedly without thinking.

When you make the choice to *shift* your *thinking*, you first need to recognize that where you are right now is a result of what you have been in the past and accept it. Take full responsibility for your past actions and release them. You then need to mindfully make a commitment to become *fully aware* of how you feel when you eat your foods. A great indicator of how you feel is your gut, or maybe your heart and chest area. During the course of your meal, ask yourself, **"How do I**

feel right now?" And answer your question. If you don't feel good, then you have the option of creating a simple but powerful affirmation to shift your current thought pattern, but this process must feel good. When you do this, you change how you perceive your delicious foods and begin to appreciate them like they were meant to be appreciated. Feeling guilty about the foods you eat brings so much negative energy into your body that you may manifest your guilt in the form of weight gain, and perhaps disease. A great way to feel even better about the foods you eat is choosing a better, healthier palate for you to enjoy. It is hard for you to feel good about what you eat if you decided to have a biggie-size value meal at McDonalds if your beliefs are not a vibrational match to your desire in regard to what you are eating. You can try to tell yourself that you feel great, but you know deeply that you are lying to yourself, and that does not feel good, either. Your goal is to feel good about the healthy foods you eat and make very special occasions to fully enjoy the foods you have a weakness or craving for. But you must enjoy the process fully!

To express full joy for the foods I eat, I start by

being Grateful and thankful for them. During the course of my meal, I often find myself going, "Mmmm, Mmmm, Mmmm," over and over again. I call it my own personal meditational eating!

Choosing to eat healthy foods is very important to your health success. Just like a small pill has a strong effect in curing a headache, every single bite of food you take has an effect on your entire body. Can you imagine this? This is how powerful and important it is that you are aware of the choice of foods you eat!

To achieve complete *awareness* in the foods you eat, you must set time aside just for eating. Avoid eating in front of the television or while doing anything else. Just focus on your delicious foods and feeling good while eating them. When you practice this, you are practicing *mindful eating*, and the results you seek for your ideal perfect body weight are just around the corner. Research has shown that it takes approximately 30 days to completely change old habits, and habits can sometimes be difficult to break, but when you make the decision to transform your life and adapt new habits for *mindful eating*, you will begin to achieve a healthy successful lifestyle.

Other affirmations I created in the past were:

-I am joyfully experiencing complete satisfaction in the healthy foods that I am eating.

-I am grateful and thankful for being my perfect weight, and it feels so good.

When I am done eating, I sometimes think back at the foods I ate, and I appreciate them even more.

I often use a wonderful and amazing mental exercise about the foods I love and crave. I sit down in a comfortable chair, I close my eyes, and I begin to visualize the foods I like the most. If I am thinking about ice cream, I may visualize a wonderful small cup of mint chocolate chip ice cream. It is beginning to melt along the sides of the cup. I take my first small bite, and I feel it melting on my tongue and touching every part of my mouth. I feel the wonderful creaminess and taste the wonderful flavor of mint. I can also taste the small bits of chocolate melting in my mouth, as they come out of nowhere. I do this process until I finish my mental cup of my favorite ice cream. When I finish this process, I open my eyes, and I feel so satisfied that I feel like I no longer need that cup of ice cream! Try this and you will experience your own little piece of heaven.

Your mind is so powerful. With it, you have the ability to create joy in everything you do. You can transform your inner suffering about the foods you eat into a joyful and satisfying healthier experience, but only you have the power to do that with the things you have learned here.

If you are struggling about choosing the right foods to eat for better health, I strongly recommend that you consult with a well-known and certified nutritionist.

You may not know this, but your body is unique and very different from everyone else's. Your nutritionist can tell you what your body type is and what foods contribute to a healthier and energy-filled lifestyle. For example, I found that I am a mixed type of food eater. I require a combination of certain fruits, vegetables, and meats. You may be a different type of food eater, like a protein type, and may require more meats to feel fulfilled, satisfied, and full of energy. Your food type is determined by your nutritionist, depending on your blood type and the results of the assessments they provide.

Exercise and the way you *think* and *feel* about exercising is equally as important to your health and success. Just like *mindful eating*, you need to be *aware* of how you *feel* when you exercise. You may connect eating and exercise very closely for success, but are you doing it the right way? We easily become guilty of eating something with the belief that it will make us gain weight, but to justify it we say to ourselves, "I am going to have to bust my butt at the gym tomorrow." Here you are creating two negative effects; feeling guilty about eating and getting punished about exercising. Think about it: as a child, when you got punished for doing something wrong, you certainly tried to remember not to do it again. What happens is that when you punish yourself for exercising, pretty soon you feel bad about going to the gym and being at the gym becomes a burden. We do this all the time, and we don't even realize it! Now every time you think about going to the gym, it does not feel good anymore and you stop going altogether. When you have this bad feeling in your gut, and you make yourself go to the gym, it is not an enjoyable experience. Why do we punish ourselves for going to the gym?

To become a healthy success, you must ask yourself, "What are the misconceptions or negative beliefs I have about going to the gym?" Going to the gym should be an exhilarating experience for you! Every time you think about going to the gym, you should feel empowered, motivated, and full of anticipation. Eliminating the bad habits about the food choices you have eliminates the guilty feeling about going to the gym. You go to the gym because you experience joy every time you go, and it makes you feel so strong and full of life. Going to the gym should make you feel like you can do anything without feeling like you have to torture yourself or feel discomfort doing it.

Mindful exercising happens when you are *aware* of how you *feel* while exercising. You take your time, you learn new exercises, you try new and different things to keep things interesting, and you do this at your own pace. *Mindful exercising* happens when you fully enjoy every routine you choose to do. You send love to every muscle group you work. Your state of mind is pure joy, you find yourself smiling while you do an arm curl, a leg press, or a 10-minute jog. I was working out one afternoon and a very nice lady approached me to ask, "You look very defined; you must exercise a lot, what is it that you do?" I replied, "I jog for 10 minutes at my own pace and do 15 reps with very low weights for any muscle group I feel like working any given day." She was astonished. Feeling good about exercising is very important to your health success. Instead of giving your body negative energy for doing something good, you empower it by mindfully filling it with good vibrating energy, by simply feeling good about doing it.

It is important to keep an *Attitude of Gratitude* about being at your perfect weight. Gratitude opens a vortex within you for manifesting more things to be thankful for. You can begin by creating Gratitude Affirmations that help you stay at the weight you want to be. Focus on it, believe it, and you will see it! *(refer to Chapter 14 to learn more about the amazing power of Gratitude)*

I find that it is very helpful to consult with a personal trainer, search online, or read health magazines about different workout routines. Change in your exercise routine keeps going to the gym very interesting. The same repetitive routines can also cause you to lose interest.

This chapter is a very important part of this book because, to be successful in every area of your life and in business, you need to feel good physically; you need to feel full of energy and vitality to joyfully empower your state of mind and success.

WHAT'S HAPPENED SINCE 2013?

In 2015, Maggie's Salsa sold with Garden Fresh to the Campbell Soup Company for $231 million dollars. Shortly after, she went back to Mexico and helped rescue 31 orphaned children from a drug cartel (as shown on page 229). As a speaker, she brings awareness about how to solve the generational issue of human sex trafficking. For more information about this movement, please visit TrueLifeHero.com.

Magie is now working with the AOF Megafest and the Hollywood Dreams International Film Festival along with Writer/Producer Harold L. Brown and Producer Del Weston to produce the story of her life for Film and Television.

She has become an International Keynote speaker, Business Coach, a Workshop Facilitator and has co-created a company with Jon Dwoskin, Adam and Jess Reilly called ConsciousKeynotes.com, a speaking agency that teaches entrepreneurs with a conscious message how to get hired as a speaker and helping them get on the stage.

TO BE CONTINUED....

REFERENCES AND RESOURCES

To learn more about the Magie Cook Company and her products and services visit:
MagieCook.com

To learn more about Dr. Masaru Emoto's work visit:
masaru-emoto.net/en/

To learn more about techniques for releasing negative beliefs, emotions and thought patterns:

The Emotional Freedom Technique
Emofree.com

The Work of Byron Katie
Thework.com

To learn more about the Silva Method and the story of Jose Silva visit:
SilvaMethod.com

To learn more about the National Science Foundation visit:
nsf.gov

Made in the USA
Middletown, DE
17 December 2021